Gladiator
Sands of Death

Matthew Sprange

Contents

Credits

Editor – Alexander Fennell

Cover Art – Anne Stokes

Interior Illustrations - Luis Corte Real, Anne Stokes, Nathan Webb, Scott Purdy, Anthea Dilly, Judy Perrin, Danilo Moretti, Brent Chumley

Additional Text – Teresa Capsey, Ian Barstow

Proof Reading – Ian Barstow

Playtesters - Harris Rotman, Rob Jones, Tommy Foster, Jim Sparling, Shannon Sparling, Jimi Braun, Michelle Braun, Jason Thornton, Teresa Scenna, Jeremy Schrage, William J. Pennington, Steve Mulhern

Special Thanks – Ridley Scott, Hans Zimmer & Lisa Gerrard, to whose work this book was written

MONGOOSE PUBLISHING

Mongoose Publishing, PO Box 1018, Swindon, SN3 1DG, United Kingdom

info@mongoosepublishing.com

Visit the Mongoose Publishing website at www.mongoosepublishing.com for regular updates.

INTRODUCTION

It is not yet mid-morning and yet the air of excitement around the grand arena is palpable. You have arrived two hours before the first matches are due to commence for the seats will fill up quickly and you have no wish to endure the sun-blasted stone benches on the south side of the arena for the whole afternoon. The crowds mill about you, all streaming for the grand arena, some mute with trepidation, other proclaiming loudly which gladiator will triumph in the matches. It has been a month since the last games day and you, along with everyone else in the city, are eager to leave behind the concerns of your everyday life, replacing it with an afternoon of fun, excitement and sheer passion.

Filing under the gigantic entrance archway of the north side, you marvel, as always, at the sheer scale of the building. It has stood in the heart of the city for hundreds of years and whilst you have been told it was constructed by mere mortals, many rumours abound of incredible sorcery and the hand of the gods themselves in its foundations. In the darkness of the great shadowy archway, dwarfed by both the size and age of this great place, it is in these rumours you put your trust.

The sun crawls across the clear sky as you make your way through the gathering crowds and into the daylight past the entrance. Before you lies the colossal sand-covered arena, banked on all sides by rows and rows of stone seating. A major residential district could comfortably rest inside the arena itself but you are well aware of the many supporting structures outside of this building – prisons, barracks, training schools, living quarters, armouries, weaponsmiths and even holding cages for incredible and magical wild creatures. The whole centre of the city has been built around the magnificent grand arena and has forever formed the core of your society. On occasion, you have heard the tales of mad and crazed travellers from other lands in taverns you visit after a toiling day's work. They sometimes speak of an even greater arena built in some nation far across the southern sea. Impossible! What could be larger than this place?

The whole crowd is herding towards the north end of the arena to claim the favoured seats and you step slowly alongside every other spectator. Everyone looks to their left, to the arena floor itself, in an effort to spy some clue as to which match will be set first. But, as always, no clue has been given, for the sand is perfectly flat and uniform. By the end of the day, it will be soaked in blood.

You finally come to a seat and are happy with your fortune, for it is right in the centre of the north end and just four tiers up – you will have a splendid, almost ringside view of the action. For the next two hours, you sit patiently with everyone else, listening to the conversations revolving around the oncoming carnage and watching the rest of the arena slowly begin to fill with spectators. There is a stir as the nobility of the city file into their shaded stand far across the arena on the west side. The first match can now only be minutes away. Vendors prowl up and down the tiers of seats, selling food and drink, though one man shoves a small parchment into your hand, the scrap proclaiming the victories and prowess of Minimus, the halfling gladiator. You have no official wagers placed today, but such information may prove useful if one of your neighbours on this tier offers a bet on his match.

A huge cheer, resounding throughout the entire arena rises incredibly with volume and your eyes are drawn to the sand where the first of the events is about to begin. The twelve men are heavily costumed but are not gladiators themselves – this is the pre-match entertainment. A small number of shows are run by the actors, mostly parodying the games themselves, though you could not help but chuckle at a satirical piece performed at the expense of Citus, a well-known noble of dubious pleasures. You try to imagine what the poor man must feel like in his expensive stand with the entire city staring and laughing at him. It is just, you decide.

The actors soon leave the sands, much to the relief of Citus no doubt, and a hush descends upon the grand arena as the crowd, thousands upon thousands of people, the entire population of the city, wait expectantly. You, and everyone else, are not silent for long as, in the centre of the nobles' stand, you spy the Lord Grelagor and his lady wife, twin rulers of the city, step forward and salute the crowd. Once more, the mob roars its approval, as much in anticipation of the coming matches as in allegiance and loyalty. At a signal from Lord Grelagor, twenty lightly armed and armoured men march on to the sands of the arena as thousands of voices, yours amongst them, continue cheering ever louder. Very soon, blood will flow.

The match is very familiar to you as all games days start this way. These are novice gladiators, either slaves or those seeking fame and fortune, desperately competing to gain the notice of the crowd. The match is short and bloody, but you focus on one woman closest to you, a lithe and well-toned figure who, although outmatched in strength by most of her opponents, adeptly avoids their blows whilst running them through with her spear. Before you know it, she is the last gladiator standing and though you try hard to catch the arena manager's announcement, you miss her name. You will certainly watch out for her later though – she may be worth a strong wager.

Bodies are cleared away by more slaves and intense conversation fills the arena as people discuss the performance and outcome of that match. Another cheer rises as the arena manager makes the announcement that Sketari and Deimos – you heard those names well enough – the famed charioteering rivals, have decided to settle who is the greatest once and for all. The midday heat is unnoticed as you immediately jump upon your seat to better see this match – chariot racing is the fastest and deadliest of all arena events. It is also your favourite. The two heavy chariots burst into the arena, sand flying up high behind them. Turning to the man standing next to you, you quickly wager three silver on Deimos. A high wager, but Deimos has long been your favoured gladiator. The blood is pumping and the adrenaline coursing through your veins – there is nothing you enjoy so much as games day.

Gladiator – Sands of Death

Gladiator is a new style of sourcebook from Mongoose Publishing, the people who brought you the acclaimed Slayer's Guides and Encyclopaedia Arcane series. This book will provide you with everything you need to know in order to integrate the world of the arena into your existing campaigns.

Part one of Gladiator – Sands of Death details the arenas themselves and the people behind them – stable masters, nobles, arena managers and, of course, the gladiators. Five fully detailed arenas are provided, ready to be slotted into any town, city, or even dungeon.

Part two brings new rules to reflect the vicious combats that take place on the sands. New and highly exotic weaponry, feats and highly specialised prestige classes will guarantee the crowd never gets bored. Expanded rules for chariots and their racing are also given alongside other, more esoteric matches. All these new rules may also be used by adventuring parties as they delve into deeper dungeons or traverse the harshest wilderness. Gladiators may work hard for the fame and glory they deserve and, possibly their freedom too. You will know your gladiator is truly one of the great attractions of the arena when he performs his first Death Move in front of a bloodthirsty crowd.

Finally, part three presents Sands of Death, a complete game based on the D20 combat system. Players each take the part of a stable master, training and grooming their gladiators in the hopes of making their fortunes within the arena. Gladiators of rival stables fight through a huge variety of matches, gradually gaining experience and skill as their stable masters continue to rake in the gold pieces from their appearances.

We who are about to die, salute you!

Lord Regupol strolled aimlessly through the malodorous maze of the slavers' dens, gold pomander of roses suspended from a jewelled handle held delicately to his nose to soften if not completely obscure the stench of humanoid suffering and close-quartered captivity. One of the women of his harem had tried to escape so he had been force to execute her and the alleged accomplices as an example to the remaining girls. Now he searched for replacements. He had already found a lovely pair of elven 'maids', fair-haired, dark-eyed beauties both, and was in search of a third girl to complete the set. He stepped gingerly over a puddle of filth to gain a closer look at a slave who had dared make eye contact. What he saw when he drew closer immediately caught his imagination and appealed to his sense of the visually absurd. To verify his vision, he motioned his eunuch to bring the elven twins closer as he inspected the human before him.

She stood slightly taller than the lord did, dark, wild hair framing a square, but somehow still attractive face in which the bluest eyes he had ever seen stared at him with total self-confidence. Her lean limbs were muscled nearly to the point of mannishness, though she was obviously quite female. This woman retained her spirit, unlike the cowering fodder around her. The vision this slave would make when paired with the two elves would delight his noble friends and make them green with envy.

Lord Regupol turned, scanning the den for the slave master. He waved his pomander and called to the loutish lump of a man who had greeted him as he wandered into the market. His inquiry was cut short by the wand of his own pomander being held tight against his throat, cutting of his air supply. He squeaked several times and batted ineffectually at the strong, feminine hands that held the bar to his throat. Darkness swam dizzying circles through his vision, distorting the hopeful faces of the elven maids, before engulfing him completely.

'Lord? My lord, are you alright?' A gruff voice emerged from the swaddling blackness, rousing Regupol. The noble opened his eyes and tried to focus on the face floating before him. 'My lord, are you awake?' The noble's eyes confirmed what his nose told him, the slaver was hovering over him, trying to revive him.

'Away brute. I am roused.' Lord Regupol waved his hand in the slaver's face and unsteadily regained his feet.

'A thousand pardons, Lord. I don't know how the wench slipped her chains. I should have warned you about her - she stole a sword and killed two of my guards on the caravan to the city.' The slaver spat through the blackened stumps of his teeth and muttered, 'Gods forsaken barbar! Nothing but trouble, first the raid, then the guards, now *this*.'

'I want her.'

The slaver blinked. 'But my lord, she tried to kill you. She is surely bound for the headsman's axe.'

'I want her. Make it so.'

The flesh monger licked his lips nervously, 'I don't see how I could possibly let her go for less than -'

Lord Regupol's hard, dark eyes bored into the slaver's face. 'You will give her to me, or I will see that it is your neck on the headsman's block.'

'I . . . but she – She'll try to kill you at the first opportunity. At every opportunity!'

Lord Regupol glared at the now unconscious and well-guarded woman. 'There will be no opportunities where she is going. As she likes to fight and kill, I will send her to a place where she will get her fill of it or die in the trying.' The noble snapped an order over his shoulder, 'Kime! Take this wench to the stable master. We'll see how well she fares in the arena.' The eunuch nodded and motioned the guards to follow him with the unconscious woman.

'Oh, and Kime, take these fool elves with you as well. I would hate to break up the set.'

Part I
Arenas and Campaigns

OVERVIEW OF THE ARENA

The arena is the centre of many societies and cultures. Based around the concept of blood sport, crowds cheer whilst those on the sands battle for life. In such games, there are no complex rules for winning and losing; it is simply kill or be killed. The victor is the one with the strength and skill to slay every opponent, to rise above the carnage with blood-stained weapon in hand to receive the adulation of a frenzied mob.

CR

Only the most debased of races seem to revel in the thrill of the arena – goblinoids, orckind and humans. Arenas in the nations of dwarves and elves are virtually unheard of, though there are many tales of gladiatorial combat taking place in the cities of the elves' dark-kin, the drow. It may not, on reflection, be so surprising that the younger races hunger for the pain and suffering of others but it is clear humans take the spectacle to the greatest heights. Whereas orcs and goblins show very little in the way of organisation in the combats they engage in for excitement and bloodlust, humans proclaim themselves sophisticated by raising immense arenas in the midst of their cities. Matches within are highly organised, as is the system behind the arena that ensures its longevity and continued supply of flesh for battle. In such civilisations, the arena is considered the highest form of entertainment. As repugnant as they may seem to a visiting dwarf or elf, there is often a far darker purpose behind the arena and, ultimately, it is not the gladiator fighting within that is the true victim, but the crowd baying for his death.

DARK DESIGNS

The greatest arenas are vast constructions by any measure, even in a world blessed by a proliferation of magic, and many are centuries, even millennia old. Whilst any border town of any pretension may build its own provincial circus in which to stage

gladiatorial matches, the resources required to even lay the foundations of a grand arena are incredible, far beyond the comprehension of the crowd that regularly attends it. Only the very greatest empires, rich in raw materials and bloated from the tribute of dozens of dominion states may even consider such an awe-inspiring structure and if these are available, it still takes a massive act of will for a ruler to commit to something of such magnitude.

There are two main reasons behind a ruler's decision to construct a grand arena. The first is a simple statement to other, rival, nations and their own rulers. By building the largest arena, indeed, what will likely be the greatest structure in the entire world, the ruler is demonstrating his power in a direct and unambiguous fashion. After all, if a nation is able to divert enough of its resources into both the construction and maintenance of a grand arena, what might it be capable of in open warfare? Grand arenas are never profitable enterprises, even in the few nations that charge their populations for attendance. Even with fifty or sixty thousand people watching the games, the immense cost of providing so many different and varied matches will drain the coffers of even an empire unless it is truly massive.

The second reason for a grand arena coming into existence is one of control – the domination of an entire population. Few empires are built with

anything other than brutality and even in a capital where the population is relatively free, trouble can arise. The greatest fear of any tyrant is that one day his power will crumble and fade. Whilst a grand arena does nothing for the military power of an empire and will drain far more gold than it brings in through increased trade, it does give everyone in the city a focus in their lives. Men and women, high and low, will talk constantly throughout the games about their favourite gladiators and the awesome events yet to be staged. Rumours become rife. It keeps them from thinking too much about abuses of political power, unfair laws, military strife on the border and the failure of corn crops. By making the grand arena the very epicentre of his capital, even the most brutal of tyrants can solidify his central

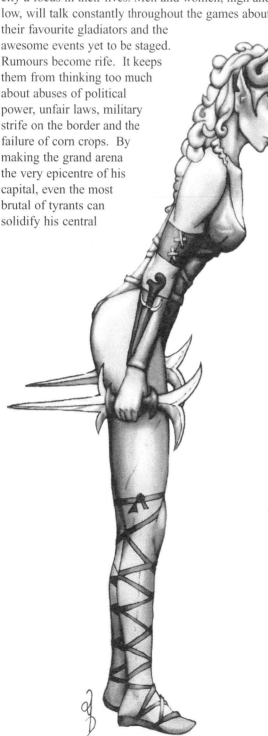

base of power and make himself all but invulnerable to his enemies, whether political or far more direct. If the games prove sufficiently spectacular, he may even gain the admiration of the population, regardless of anything else he does.

It is, perhaps, an irony that the fulcrum of such concerns of political and empirical might rests on a relatively small handful of men and women. The presence of a grand arena may impact an entire empire and hold tens of thousands in absolute awe, but the entertainment provided comes from a select number of individuals – the gladiators.

GLADIATORS

There is forever a great deal of speculation and interest concerning those who dare walk into the arena and catch the imagination of thousands. To a visitor from another nation, the gladiator can appear as a god, ruthlessly slaying his enemies and swaying the opinion of the crowd with a mere sword thrust. The truth, as always, is a little different.

The vast majority of gladiators in a grand arena are slaves – they have to be for there is simply no way to convince huge numbers of freemen to enter the arena voluntarily. During special occasions and anniversaries, games can easily run for over one hundred consecutive days and lead to the deaths of ten thousand gladiators. Clearly, providing gladiators for the arena is an industry in itself and this is exactly what arises in any city with a grand arena. Slaves for the games may be criminals once rotting in prison, captured enemy prisoners of war or simply brought into the city as trade in slave trains. In a few empires, slaves may also be bred specifically to fight in the arena, their owners constantly on the lookout for strength and speed.

Many receive little or no training in the weapons and armour they are given, their only purpose to provide the sight of slaughter for a bloodthirsty crowd. From the ranks of these poor wretches, a handful will emerge who are fitter and eminently more willing to kill than the others and these are the ones their owners will lavish attention on. They receive specialised training for the matches their owner wishes to compete in and better accommodation. They will also begin to get paid, typically 5-20% of the winnings gained from their matches, by order of the city's ruler. A slave earning relatively large sums of gold is far less likely to rebel than one used only to hardship and rulers are all too aware of the dangers posed by a gladiator revolt, for their combat prowess will have been witnessed first hand in the arena. The amount a slave earns for appearances varies with the generosity of the city's ruler but it is possible for them to hoard enough gold to buy their freedom from their owners within five to ten years. This lure of money has even resulted in freemen, especially fighters, actually selling themselves into slavery in the blind hope of gaining or rebuilding a fortune. It is perhaps an obvious fact that few, slaves or freemen alike, ever live to see such dreams come to fruition. The arena is splattered with the blood of too many fallen gladiators for their hopes to be realistic.

The average life expectancy of a gladiator is just one match – most are slain in their very first appearance, the odds skewed against them as matches for new arrivals are often sheer carnage, meat grinds to separate the potential greats from the rest of the rabble. If a gladiator is able to live through a dozen matches, his chances of survival increase dramatically, for by this time he has become hardened to the killing and has begun to learn the fighting skills needed.

Something else also begins to happen at this time – the crowd will start to recognise his name and expect to see a good show whenever he appears. The most successful gladiators of all are not those who are merely able to slay every opponent they face, but those who can engage the crowd and capture the imagination of the mob. Experienced gladiators learn to work the crowd by adopting unusual mannerisms or weapon combinations, and by demonstrating incredible flair and bravery as they fight. Whenever these champions set foot upon the sands, the cheering of thousands is deafening. It is not long before this adulation becomes the main focus of the gladiator's life, far more so than money or even freedom. Revelling in glory, he begins to live for the roar of the crowd and, in so doing, makes himself ever more popular. Such men and women may soon come to consider themselves invulnerable.

STABLE MASTERS

The key figure in the life of every gladiator is his owner, the stable master. Such men are usually either wealthy nobles or ex-gladiators who managed to find their fortune and freedom. By a process of bidding and bribery, they are able to obtain contracts from the grand arena that allow them to enter gladiators into matches and be paid for doing so.

They will then begin to buy worthy-looking slaves and equip them for the initial matches. Many look upon the stable masters as callous flesh merchants, willing to trade in pain and suffering for gold.

Whilst a stable master must, indeed, retain a certain detachment, especially with new and untrained slaves, it is very common for an

attachment to form with favoured gladiators. Whilst there will always be a sharp division between slave and master, it is a stronger relationship than a knight may have with a favoured warhorse and this comes as something of a surprise for many not aware of what exactly goes on within the gladiator stables. Stable masters who were once gladiators themselves are often seen growing relationships with their slaves and whilst they are likely to be just as hard and punishing on a physical level, no doubt due to their own experiences from the past, they also tend to train and groom their slaves as proteges rather than mere sources of income.

Rivalries abound amongst different stables and their masters as a loss for one in the arena is a financial gain for another. Underhanded tricks and ploys abound between them but most would readily agree that it is not rival stable masters that cause the most problems but the arena manager.

Arena Managers & Contracts

The arena manager enjoys a position of immense prestige, status and wealth within the grand arena and is likely to be of noble birth, appointed by the city ruler himself. His main duties revolve around the actual day-to-day running of the arena and as such must always ensure enough gladiators are available, that beasts and monsters are rare and exotic enough, the pre-match entertainment sufficiently amusing, the vendors present for serving food and yet not charging too much – the list of his responsibilities is endless. If he is successful, the games will run smoothly and the crowd will be entertained. Failure will result in immediate dismissal and banishment from noble society – a lot of the empire's gold rests on his own personal abilities.

Games days typically take place in the grand arena every week or every month, but special games to commemorate great events may last many consecutive days and always place a great strain on the resources an arena manager has at his disposal. Gladiators themselves tend to be the most sought after commodity, for thousands will be needed for such events. To guarantee demand is met, arena managers institute a system of contracts for stable masters. The benefit to the stable master is that he may freely purchase slaves and be guaranteed a return in gold for every one he puts into the arena.

The downside is that the contract is incredibly binding and weighted purely in favour of the arena. When demand is made for gladiators to compete in the nightmarish meat grind of a re-enacted battle, the stable master has no choice but to comply, even if it means potentially losing a favoured gladiator he has been nurturing.

A great deal of negotiation and manoeuvring takes place every games day as stable masters constantly try to find a better deal for themselves, usually at the expense of a rival. Most attempts are doomed to failure but a canny stable master always offers something in return – arena managers tend to be extremely well paid, so straight forward bribery rarely works. On the other hand, they also tend to be very paranoid about putting on a stunning show, or spectacle as it is sometimes called, and its effect on their continued position. More than one stable master has been able to keep his gladiators out of the carnage of a battle by promising to provide some exotic and magical creature for a match.

The Supporting Cast

Aside from the individuals detailed above, there are literally thousands of others required to keep the grand arena in operation during a games day – stonemasons, farmers, beast handlers, cartwrights, slaves, merchants, guards, vendors, noble patrons, labourers and healers to name just a few. The grand arena is an industry in and of itself and the economy of the capital is built around its presence.

Wizards and sorcerers are kept in constant employment by the grand arena and serve a wide variety of functions. Those less skilled with powerful magicks may join the pre-match entertainment, delighting the crowd with brilliant light displays or sorcerous energies and loud but harmless explosions. Whilst this is often felt as demeaning the art by some, the grand arena rarely shows any compassion to those it uses.

Mages also keep watch for items of magical power smuggled on to the sands of the arena by gladiators desperate for any advantage. Magically charged weapons and armour are viewed with great suspicion by arena managers for such things may alter the course of a match, or bring about its end far too soon. Theirs is the business of entertainment and any gladiator found attempting to employ magic in a match is likely to be fined, humiliated or even executed as a lesson to others.

provide nightmare creatures from the infernal planes that the spectators have truly never witnessed before.

THE MOB

The greatest consideration for any involved in the running of the grand arena, not least for the city's ruler, is the actual population, the crowd that lines the ranked tiers around the sands or, as some nobles cynically call them, the mob.

The fundamental purpose of the grand arena is to amuse the crowd, capture their popular imagination and by doing so, force them to think about the gladiators rather than ordinary day-to-day concerns that could so easily cause problems for the ruler. The crowd gambles and wagers on the outcome of matches and debates rage on who is the finest gladiator or which is the better combination of weapons and armour. Children emulate gladiators in the street as their parents pay silver and gold for busts or statues of their favourite combatants. In a city ruled by the iron hand of an imperial dictator, few are permitted to rise above their immediate station and so hopes and dreams find their escape in the actions of the gladiator champion who succeeds time and again within the arena.

The presence of mages is most notable in the games themselves though. Whilst it is relatively rare for them to enter as gladiators themselves, their ability to raise or lower huge stone walls, create fog out of thin air and hinder or slow gladiators who might otherwise have too great an advantage over an opponent, is well-employed by the arena manager. Even darker magicks may be trivialised and used for the entertainment of the crowd. Slain gladiators may both walk and fight once more with the presence of a necromancer and a demonologist can

Brawls in taverns can erupt when the population feels a gladiator has been unfairly treated and many experience grief when their favoured is slain, actually entering into a period of mourning as if a member of their own family had died. The irony that a mere slave can cause such feelings in an entire population is not lost on the scholars who deign to study the effects of the grand arena, rather than merely cheer with bloodlust with the rest of the mob.

SMALLER ARENAS

The grand arena is by no means the only venue in which gladiators fight. In an empire with a grand arena in the heart of its capital, it is an inevitability that the smaller towns of the outlying provinces will try their best to emulate the spectacle. Any town of sufficient self-importance will begin the construction of its own arena, a far cry from that of the capital in both size and scope, but a close enough approximation for a population destined never to see the grand arena for themselves.

Such places are where many stable masters begin their careers and though matches tend to be far less sophisticated, they are no less deadly for the gladiators themselves. The more expensive matches, such as beast fights and chariot races will be absent altogether and games days themselves will come more rarely but the crowds attending miss little – the fundamental principles of bloodshed and slaughter are still present, no matter how little thought and gold go behind them.

The most interesting phenomenon revolving around the crowd, however, is their effect upon the matches themselves. Gladiator champions quickly learn to get the crowd on their side whenever they enter the arena, a process greatly speeded by their own fame through countless victories, as well as judicious advertising on the part of their stable master. When a crowd howls and chants the name of a gladiator, he will feel the effect of thousands of minds, all wishing, praying even, for his success. His sword strokes and spear thrusts become more accurate and powerful, even as his opponent is weakened by the knowledge that the mob is demanding his own death. The effect is marked and the outcome of many matches can actually be influenced by the crowd in this manner. Some liken this to the morale boost troops in battle gain from being led by a great hero, whilst others believe it is the will of the immortal gods that make the wishes of their faithful manifest. Once again, it is left to the scholars to debate such issues – the mob neither knows nor cares. They only wish to see great carnage and the flow of blood on each and every games day.

Away from the great empires, large arenas are far less common, for they are expensive to run and without a population requiring constant suppression, many of the reasons for their existence are absent. Individual city states may build smaller arenas within their walls, though such places tend to be run for pure profit and slavery may be outlawed altogether. These two factors result in far less spectacular matches and hence, a reduced popularity, especially as the freemen fighting generally prefer to battle to the first wound, rather than death.

Whatever the shape and form, from the largest grand arena to the most squalid pit fight, it seems likely that the continued fascination with death and pain of the younger races will ensure the existence of such places. Arenas represent the pinnacle of brutality within a civilisation, but also hope for the mob, the stable masters and even the gladiator slave who dreams of his eventual freedom.

RACES OF THE SPECTACLE

Almost every sentient race in the world has walked on to the sands of death as a gladiator, be they freemen, captives or slaves. Arena managers are forever seeking new and exotic combatants to retain the interest of the crowd but there are favourites both readily available and in possession of the ability to contribute to the spectacle being built in each day of the games.

HUMANS

Alone of all the races, it is the human that possess the greatest flexibility in terms of both skill and adaptability. The vast majority of arenas are also built in human dominated cities and thus it is far easier for the crowd to relate to their favoured gladiator. Being the most numerous of all races ensures a steady supply for even the lowliest stable master and arena managers are far more prepared to risk a human in new matches of their devising than a harder to obtain humanoid.

As gladiators, humans can turn their abilities to almost any combatant role in the arena and only be outmatched by other races in a few areas of speed and endurance, but rarely both. Their penchant for blood-letting and strife is also a bonus to the crowd, for there are few peoples capable of more outright savagery than the short-lived humans.

DWARVES

Though at a serious disadvantage in matches requiring speed and agility, dwarves are rock solid warriors able to sustain incredible amounts of damage that would floor a being of another race. Those gambling on the outcome of matches always weigh odds very carefully when a dwarf steps into the arena for their sturdiness and fortitude is renowned.

Stable masters often work hard to procure several dwarves amongst their gladiators for whilst their combat capabilities are beyond reproach, they often have a hard time fighting alongside any not of their own race. Their known antagonism towards elves can spell the disruption of a complete stable with duels and brawls putting gladiators out of action before they can even reach the arena, much to the chagrin of their owners. A stable master is often left hoping the damage caused is paid for by the dwarf's winnings in his next match. It should also be noted that dwarves are renowned for making very poor chariot drivers. Whilst their slightly smaller size

does indeed aid them in taking cover from an opponent's blows whilst in the chariot itself, they have little or no affinity towards horses and their control, an essential characteristic for any good driver.

ELVES

The slight form of an elf entering the arena can sometimes be accompanied by howls of derision from the mob. Shorter than humans and with a build seemingly too fragile for the rigours of intense combat, they do however possess a natural quickness and dexterity that enables them to dodge the lumbering blows of others, and then strike with deadly accuracy.

When permitted to engage in matches that allow them to fight autonomously with little regard for allies, they are at their best. An elf allowed to

choose his own ground within the arena and use his natural talents can be a terrible foe to face. When physically restricted in some way, however, an elf loses many advantages to more flexible races, such as humans.

GNOMES AND HALFLINGS

Human dominated arenas often group halflings and gnomes together as gladiators, with the ignorant often incorrectly naming one as the other – to the mob, they all look alike. Enterprising arena managers often put on comedy matches, with many poorly armed and trained halflings and gnomes thrown into combat against a much larger monster. This is one of the crueller matches one may see in an arena.

A very small number of halflings and gnomes, however, learn to fight on almost equal terms against the larger gladiators. They give much ground in terms of strength with their best blows sometimes almost completely ineffective against the arena champions. Their typically gentle temperament is also a hindrance to the bloody work of fighting but the rare breed amongst both race may gain, through years of pitiless slavery, a harder edge, a desire to achieve freedom and a passion for killing. Such gladiators manage to find they do indeed possess advantages others do not. They are immediately underestimated whenever walking on to the sands, sometimes leading to a fatal overconfidence in their opponents. Their small size can also be utilised to dodge the blows of their enemies. If properly trained in speed and accuracy, a halfling or gnome may well become respected as a gladiator in their own right, even if they are unlikely to become true champions.

GOBLINOIDS

The goblinoid races are a common sight in many arenas for they are numerous in the world and easily fit into the role of villainous gladiators for the crowd to despise. Spectators are always keen to see races so very different from themselves and yet rarely bother with the distinctions between each goblinoid. Arena managers and stable masters are very much aware of the differences between goblins, hobgoblins and bugbears, however.

Goblins are captured relatively easily for use in the arena and may thus be used in large numbers. They are cowardly and sneaky creatures that must always be watched whilst in captivity, but they make ideal hordes for the battles staged in the arena. Arena managers may also set goblins against halflings and gnomes as an amusing mid-afternoon diversion for the crowd.

Hobgoblins are another matter entirely and this race can produce very good gladiators indeed. Their love of combat and own maintenance of weapons and armour make them a great choice for stable masters willing to gain the reputation for training evil combatants. Hobgoblins often enjoy life as a gladiator and most quickly forget they are enslaved when they begin to earn huge amounts of gold for work they ordinarily consider a worthwhile pastime.

As the largest and most powerful of the goblinoids, bugbears make for fearsome gladiators in the arena. They are, however, hard to train and stable masters often find the need to treat them with a great deal of respect. Gold will keep a bugbear content for a while, as will the ruthless killing of the arena but, ultimately, they always become bored and frustrated with their captivity.

ORCS AND HALF-ORCS

There have been many famous orc and half-orc gladiators over the centuries, becoming the villains the mob loves to hate. As renowned as goblinoids for being the evil barbarians of the wastes that forever plague civilisation with their raiding, there exists a certain satisfaction amongst those within the cities at seeing such creatures fight and die for their entertainment. The unfortunate effect of this is that half-orcs are seen only as brute monsters with little use or value outside of the arena. Those entering such a city are likely to be quickly captured, enslaved and made into gladiators.

Orcs make for capable, if unsophisticated, gladiators and may even come to enjoy both the work and the rewards. A half-orc may possess many of the traits that make humans such good gladiators but they are rarely treated any differently to full-blooded orcs. Any humanity they may possess is quickly eroded by the trials forced upon them.

OTHER RACES

In the constant search for bigger and better games, together with any ruler's wish to outdo and outspend his predecessors, arena managers are forced to constantly devise new matches and locate never before seen gladiators. The list of sentient races that have been forced into slavery for the games is almost endless but there are a few which have become firm favourites with the crowd over the years.

The more common humanoid races such as kobolds and gnolls are regular features in arenas able to procure a reliable source, usually from adventurers or other glory-seekers, but for all the entertainment they provide, kobolds individually make very poor fighters and gnolls have a tendency to enter blood-crazed rages when enslaved themselves. Giants are also sought after as few people ever see them outside the arena and matches involving such a huge and powerful race are always stunning to witness. One popular type of match pits a single giant against several axe-wielding dwarves.

Races of the deep earth can prove extraordinarily difficult to capture for work in the arena and few are well-suited to fighting in the bright light of the surface world anyway. The incredible fighting skill and natural abilities of races such as the drow, however, have sometimes kept crowds amused on otherwise miserable, overcast days.

THE ARENAS

Throughout the worlds of fantasy, there is a staggering array of arenas. Some are no better than small pits set in the basements of the most disreputable of establishments, where low-life warriors and rogues engage in brutal fights to the death for just a few silver coins. Others are huge affairs, grander even than the real-life Roman colosseum and dominating the city built around them as they house every kind of gladiator known. Whatever their size and grandeur, all arenas serve the same purpose – to provide the most bloodthirsty of entertainment for an audience jaded and dispirited with their ordinary, mundane lives.

Five example arenas are presented here, all of varying sizes and complexity. Full backgrounds are provided for each, allowing a Games Master to either simply 'drop' them into any existing campaign as he sees fit, or modify them to suit specific towns and cities of the nations his Player Characters travel within. Alternatively, any of the arenas may be used as the basis of a Sands of Death game, featured on p64.

PIT FIGHTS

In every walk of life there are those who simply do not fit in. For whatever reason, they are below the law. The world of gladiatorial combat is no different and whilst most arenas, large and small, fulfil important duties with regards to keeping the populace content and entertained, there are some that go unregulated, their prime purpose being to provide hardened gamblers with the ultimate in high-stakes wagering. Like so many underbellies, pit fights are looked upon with disdain by haughty stable masters who frequent the great arenas of the world. Many may have conveniently forgotten their own roots. . .

THE STRUTTING WENCH

Tylos Gart's tavern, The Strutting Wench, is on the outside no different to a thousand other wayside taverns. Warm, inviting and comfortable, it invites the passing visitor to tie his mount up and rest the night in comfort. Seemingly normal in every way, it is the perfect front for the tavern's alternate business.

Tylos has been a pit fight master for most of his adult life, having followed in his father's footsteps,

and he acquired The Strutting Wench precisely because of its location. Having already been driven out of two towns for arranging pit fights, Tylos wanted an establishment a little further from civilised settlements and he found what he was looking for at the Strutting Wench.

The pit fight master looks for an innocuous property, without an overly-large clientele, and with the particular facilities necessary for staging pit fights. Specifically, the tavern needs a large underground area available to hold the actual fights, perhaps a cellar or small set of caves, and it is the latter which attracted Tylos to The Strutting Wench. Built on the roadside against a steep crag for protection against the harsh north winds, the builder took advantage of the natural rock caves at the rear and beneath to turn it into a large and rather splendid wine cellar.

The tavern had been doing poorly when Tylos arrived to take it off the hands of the pleasantly surprised innkeeper. He closed it for nearly two months whilst the appropriate alterations were made. First, the overly-large cellar was effectively separated into three sections, with the smallest area, nearest to the descending stairs, retained for wine. With a false door built into the racks, Tylos began to construct the major part of his business enterprise. His workers dug into the stone floor and a square pit, measuring fifteen feet per side was sunk seven feet into the ground below. After this, at the very rear of the caves far from any inquisitive ears, a small holding area little more than a wooden cage was constructed, into which the more involuntary combatants of the pit fight were intended to be kept.

From the bottom of the cellar stairs, a visiting patrol would have no idea that a thriving pit fight ring is in operation mere feet from them. The hidden door is easily concealed with various bottles breaking up any suggestions of an uneven surface and rush matting on the floor concealing any tell-tale footprints. Behind the door the atmosphere changes, even when the pit is unoccupied. Lining the edges of the pit itself are all manner of protruding spikes – bones, stakes, and old weapon blades, designed of course, to keep any unwilling contestants within. Surrounding the pit are a number of wooden benches with spaces in the middle of the northern and southern sides for the fighters to enter the arena. These are the only unprotected sections and the

Opening the solid front door of the tavern, Aramor, noted seller of fine herbs, was too busy shaking the excess rain from his cloak and hat to notice the anticipation on many of the faces in the room at his arrival. He trudged wearily to the bar where the landlord was quietly fingering a wooden mug. Odd how all tavern keepers seemed to do the same when they had nothing better to do, he thought.

'Good evening, traveller,' said the landlord in greeting.

'Oh, good evening,' Aramor replied, too wet and miserable to notice the barman's coolly appraising stare.

'A drink?' ventured the tavern keeper, his eyes imperceptibly looking past Aramor and flickering to another man, sitting quietly at a small table.

'Please,' replied Aramor. 'Hot wine, perchance?'

The barman nodded, turning to a still-steaming cauldron. 'Freshly made, sir.'

Aramor took the filled mug gratefully, inhaling the sweet aroma. 'How much?' he enquired.

'Don't worry, sir. We'll settle up later. You'll be staying, I assume?' Aramor didn't know the half of it. 'Perhaps you'd like to sit over by the fire in the corner and get yourself warm.'

Aramor nodded, clutching the hot mug in both hands. Glancing about, he saw that against one of the walls near the fire was a particularly comfortable-looking chair. It struck him as a bit odd that such a chair would go unused but when he looked about the tavern, the half-dozen or so regulars studiously ignored him. Returning the compliment, he sank himself into the chair.

Staring deeply into the cup, Aramor took several sips, allowing his mind to wander. What would prices be like in the next town? Would there be a friendly guild on hand to help him trade? Lost in thought, he was just remembering his faithful mule outside when he thought he heard a gentle grating sound behind him. Odd, he thought, as the chair began tipping backwards of its own accord.

He woke up later to the noise of a group of men arguing. He couldn't make out what it was they were arguing about and when he struggled up to a sitting position, he found that one of his legs was manacled to the dirt wall behind him. Realisation began to sink in and with it came panic. He didn't know why he was suddenly a chained captive, but none of the possibilities seemed good ones.

'Where in the name of the gods am I?' Aramor yelled, his courage welling slightly at the sound of his own voice. The arguing stopped at once and footsteps sounded, coming towards him.

A man came around the corner of what looked to be the approaches to a cellar and smiled coldly at the herb seller. 'You're awake then? About time.'

'Look, if it's money you want,' Aramor began, 'Then I - '

' - Have none,' finished the man. 'More to the point, can you use a sword?'

'A sword? Of course not. What do I look like?'

'Dead meat,' said the man.

fighters either jump or are thrown bodily into the pit. There are no grand entrances to be made here. The walls of the cellar remain as they were when they housed only wine, with the addition of a few extra torches to play a shadowed light across the bloodthirsty proceedings.

Upstairs in the tavern, the only work needed was to a section of the wall directly over the holding cage below. A secret opening was built into the wall and the most comfortable chair in the tavern rigged up against it. On the floor at another table nearby, always occupied by one of Tylos' henchmen, a covert foot switch releases the wall trigger, sliding the chair backwards and depositing the unfortunate occupant down into the pit. With a less than twenty foot drop, most survive to die in a more spectacular way later.

The advantages Tylos has at The Strutting Wench over his previous ventures are all primarily down to location. A dozen miles north and south to the nearest towns, he benefits both from regular stopovers and comfort of distance from those civilised folk who may blanche at the pit fighting enterprise. He is also now fully independent, owing no tithes to the thieves' guilds and professional extortionists who control the pit fights and other nefarious activities that go on within more formal communities.

The modus operandi at The Strutting Wench is gloriously straightforward. Having set up his business, Tylos personally travelled to both the local towns, frequenting the taverns and determining whether any pit fight operation was already in existence. He discovered two important pieces of information; first, there were indeed no rival set-ups neighbouring him, and second, like everywhere else, these men of the north had a taste for gambling. He already knew them to be a violent and unsympathetic people. Perfect for his needs.

The staff – remarkably few – were in place quickly. All the old keeper's people were politely told their services would no longer be required, although one senior barman did have to be removed with a hatchet, and Tylos recruited his own people. His trusted lieutenant, Korsk, is responsible for the operation of the trap door and he also makes sure the two thugs used as security during pit fight bouts are kept in fighting condition themselves.

Korsk also acts as Tylos' book-keeper, organising betting and earning a cut of the winnings. The regulars bet on anything related to the pit fights, from the time taken for first blood to the number of visible wounds on a corpse. This suits Tylos just fine as it means that he can use victims of all shapes and sizes, rather than just those suited for fighting. That said, the biggest treat for his punters still comes from proper gladiatorial matches, either held between two local toughs fighting for prize money or, alternatively, when a renowned pit fighter arrives in the locale, challenging all-comers to defeat him.

ORC CAVERN ARENAS

Humans are by no means the only race to have discovered the joys of the spectacle. Other humanoid races, and in particular orcs, have developed a taste for the blood-soaked entertainment and have adapted it to their own way of life. Deep within their tribal caverns, these creatures have learnt to thrill at the sight of captured travellers and adventurers ruthlessly fighting those who were their former companions, in the desperate hope that survival will perhaps earn them a reprieve on their own doomed existence. This can be a most ignoble finale for an adventuring party, becoming the playthings of the very creatures they have looked upon with such disdain in the past.

BALDROG'S CAVERN

When Baldrog, the orcish chieftain of the Foot Cutter tribe, was captured in battle against a human army, none of his followers expected to see him again. A new chieftain forced his way to the summit, and life continued much as it always had. Baldrog was quickly forgotten as he was taken to the town of his conquerors, expecting a swift execution. It came as no little surprise when he was anatomically examined by a veritable grandfather before being moved again, this time to become gladiator.

Baldrog knew what gladiators were, of course. He knew humans loved to watch others fighting – to the death, he presumed – rather than be forced to do it themselves. He had always regarded it as a weakness, yet as soon as he strode into his first arena match, Baldrog became hooked on the accompanying adrenaline rush. It also turned out that he was rather good at it. However, Baldrog refused to be anybody's entertainment. He still had grand plans of his own.

After many years, Baldrog finally managed to slay the trainer to whom he had been assigned and made his escape. Making slow passage back to his original tribal lands, Baldrog naively assumed he would be welcomed back as chieftain immediately. However, life had moved on for the Foot Cutters, and Grourk, the new chieftain, had no intention of relinquishing power to a dead orc. Unfortunately for the new leader, Baldrog had developed from a notable fighter into a superb one. Whereas once before a number of his lieutenants had previously considered challenging him for leadership of the Foot Cutters, it rapidly became apparent that the returning orc was very different to the chieftain they had once known. Using tricks he had mastered on the sands of death, Baldrog ruthlessly butchered Grourk and in doing so impressed upon his subjects just how capable a warrior he had become.

The intention had been merely to regain his dominant tribal position, but Baldrog's display made a strong impact upon the Foot Cutters. They wanted to know how he had learnt to fight so well and, more than that, they had enjoyed the display as it had possessed a showmanship they had never before witnessed. In the past, a duel between two orcs had been over and forgotten as soon as a victor emerged, but Baldrog had made a lasting impression and it was one not lost on him. He began to wonder exactly why the human nobles provided gladiators for their subjects. Was it to keep them satisfied and content? Might such an arena not work for the orcs below him as well? It was not as great a leap of orcish logic as might be imagined. Baldrog had smelt the excitement on his orcs and it was far more intense than he had scented before. Raw animal instinct could be just as sharp as the keenest mind.

Accordingly, Baldrog set his mind to turning the strongest of his Orcs into gladiators. Calls for volunteers went unanswered. He knew that to press his own tribe too hard would be folly but fortunately an answer readily presented itself when a party of adventurers were captured trying to invade the Foot

Cutters' territory. Normally they would simply have been tortured but Baldrog saw a rare opportunity. Of the five prisoners, one proved to be a wizard and was slain out of hand for fear his magical powers would prove too great for the orcs to imprison. The other four all seemed to know how to fight but they were friends and steadfastly refused to co-operate with Baldrog's idea for arena combat once they found out the orc's intent. At first Baldrog was frustrated for to make this work as he planned, he needed the adventurers to fight. It took four days without food and continual, though ultimately worthless, promises of freedom for any emerging victor but eventually Baldrog had four potential gladiators prepared to fight one another. Led down into the great cavern where the orcs held council, a rough circle of shielded warriors were formed into the approximation of an arena by Baldrog himself.

Two of the would-be combatants, a dwarf and an elf, still resisted the bestial concept of gladiatorial combat and balked at the prospect of fighting so Baldrog sagely pitted each against one of the humans. The humans, it turned out, were the most easily swayed into fighting their past comrades and their aspirations towards noble conduct fell far short of the haughty elf and the austere dwarf. Neither human made it past their first fight. The poor light of the cavern gave the dwarf and elf too great an advantage over them. Both dwarf and elf quickly grasped that to remain passive was to invite death at the hands of a supposed friend and instinct began to take over as they fought desperately in front of their captors, shadows flickering back and forth behind them, magnified against the cavern walls. That the dwarf went on to slay the elf in the final match meant little to Baldrog. It was the effect it had upon the Foot Cutters which gratified him.

In the aftermath of this first fight, Baldrog began to improve his cavern arena somewhat. Still used as the main meeting hall for the Foot Cutters, the place changes dramatically when a gladiatorial match is due. In a parody of the great human arenas, sand was scattered across the rock floor and the hunting skins on the walls replaced by poor orc artistry of successful gladiators, painted directly onto the rock in the blood of their victims. In pride of place still endures the picture of the unnamed dwarf who won the first match and was then ritually burnt to death the following day. Even Baldrog could not conceive that the dwarf had actually believed him about attaining freedom.

THE SPREAD OF ORC CAVERN ARENAS

Unlike the humans, the notion of gladiatorial entertainment is not one that naturally springs to the orcish mind. It is not that they cannot find the sight of killing entertaining, far from it. The race simply lacks the artistic imagination needed to convert death into entertainment of any degree of sophistication. Occasionally, former orc gladiators have returned to their tribes with wild tales of the arena but not all fare as well as Baldrog. However, word amongst orcs spreads fast and soon members of other tribes were visiting the Foot Cutters to see for themselves the arena he had constructed. Before long, they began to bring prisoners of their own to challenge whoever the Foot Cutters themselves had to offer. On very rare occasions, Baldrog himself donned his old armour and took to the arena himself, to demonstrate to other orc tribes the fighting style of which they had heard. The picture of the half-elf who finally managed to slay him joined the others on the cavern walls.

Baldrog's own death, however, did nothing to slow down the spread of cavern fighting. Whereas before visiting orc tribes had been somewhat in awe of the ageing gladiator, they now felt no constraints about using their own caverns to expand the entertainment. Before long, a vast network of underground gladiatorial arenas sprang up, each with the traditional sand floor and wall paintings made famous by Baldrog. The bouts themselves rarely deviate much from the original concept and invariably captured adventurers fight one another for the promise of extended life and eventual freedom. They are all doomed, however, for orcs have little wish to keep such dangerous prisoners for long and so the victor is rarely allowed to survive a match, no matter how hard he has fought.

THE PROVINCIAL CIRCUS

Whilst every gladiator may imagine himself striding powerfully out into one of the great city arenas of the world, most spend their entire, and often short, careers performing in the provincial circuses which litter the nations of mankind. These small arenas fulfil a vital communal role, often acting as a multi-purpose site; meeting place, entertainment venue and governmental building. Unlike the greater arenas, most provincial circuses are owned by the

Ruzman sat impassively in the wooden barracks block, taking in the sounds of the arena beyond the simple double doors out of sight along the angled corridor. He looked carelessly about, eyeing up his stable-mates. No two were armed identically, a mark of his stable master Zuabir, and it made him reconsider his own equipment, calmly checking it over as he had been taught to do. The steamy local weather dictated a minimal amount of clothing and Ruzman wore only a short kilt in addition to his fighting equipment. This consisted of a chainmail sleeve on his right arm, attached to his torso by leather straps, light iron greaves, a long thrusting spear and a three-headed bolas. He wore no helmet, which rather pleased him as he always considered he had a rather formidable profile. The spear would keep opponents at arm's length anyway.

Ruzman stood up dutifully as one of Zuabir's slaves came over to oil his body. It was a standard part of the act, improving the appearance of the gladiator and making him far harder to grapple. He studiously ignored the tendering slave – there was a pecking order everywhere, even in gladiatorial stables.

Having been fully anointed, Ruzman sat down, twirling the bolas nonchalantly whilst he considered his particular bout. His opponent would already be on the sand, he had been told. Unlike the arenas where the gladiators came out from opposite tunnels, here the simple design meant that the fighters of the other school were only a wooden wall away, and it was considered improper for them to walk out side by side. Nobody wanted to take the risk of the fight being over before the public might actually see it.

He smiled at the thought, wondering if it had ever happened. It mattered not. Surprise was the constant companion of the professional gladiator and Ruzman knew he could live with it. He had a natural aptitude with the bolas and he was certain few other fighters would be experienced in facing them. That would be his decisive advantage, of course.

A great cheer from outside told him that one of his predecessors had succumbed and he stood up unhesitatingly, knowing he was the next into the arena. The applause began to die down and Ruzman heard the faint sound of Syman announcing his imminent arrival in the arena as he sensed an attendant approaching him. He followed the man's motion and walked into the surprisingly narrow corridor. They probably couldn't get two fighters abreast here if they wanted to. As the doors opened ahead of him, he shut his eyes briefly to prevent the brilliant daylight from blinding him. Stepping into the arena, he acknowledged the cheers of the crowd with a more flamboyant twirl of the bolas.

Less than a minute later Osric stomped away back towards the barracks. He couldn't wait to get away from the foetid heat of the arena. As he walked his foot struck against something and he looked down, slightly puzzled. Then he smiled. Bolas! What idiot would use those?

town in which they stand, with an arena master handling the daily affairs of the venue. As such, the gladiatorial facilities are less specialised than those found in the larger arenas and this can greatly limit the nature of the games held.

SYMAN'S AMPHITHEATRE

The amphitheatre managed by Syman is typical of those circuses which serve the parochial populaces of the world. The structure itself is primarily wooden, elliptical in design and with one open end. The seating is almost wholly natural, the design being built around a naturally tiered rock formation which provides banked seating for the crowds. A specially constructed and covered enclosure for the nobility is centrally located at the front of the curved rock seating.

When the town was first founded, the elders met in this natural court and, over time, it became the hub of the settlement, requiring constant improvements to befit its growing status. Behind the rising tiers, an outlining wooden wall was constructed to mirror the natural shape, with a squared gateway constructed at the apex, necessitating a wide flight of steps to be built on the external approach. Due to the almost perpetually fine weather in this broiling land, a roof was considered an unnecessary luxury. Initially this adaptation was thought satisfactory but with the arrival of gladiatorial combat, it became

clear the arena would need to undergo major improvements. A fully enclosed barracks was constructed along one side where the gladiators themselves would be housed. Opposite, a series of holding cells were built, designed to keep either prisoners or wild creatures as the need arose. A six foot palisade was also added to separate the crowd from the gladiators, necessitating many spectators to stand up in order to see the combats taking place. The crowd have taken to bringing their own awnings with them on games days, created from a colourful farrago of materials raised up on canes, adding a unique dimension to the circus of which both Syman and his noble employers approve. With the arena complete, the town now had a fine circus, shaped like a slightly irregular and incomplete oval.

With a plethora of sand nearby, it was decided to cover the natural grass to enhance the atmosphere, as well as to facilitate the cleaning and maintenance of the arena. Two rival stable masters were brought in from one of the city arenas for the inaugural three-day spectacle, which sadly turned into a one-afternoon affair when the first fourteen paired fighters escaped through the open end, easily slaughtering the inexperienced members of the civic militia posted to stop such an occurrence.

It was considerably easier to round up fleeing gladiators than it was to come up with a satisfactory answer to this new problem. The obvious resolution, namely to fully encircle the site, was rejected due to the relative softness of the ground. It was at this

point that Syman, the current arena master, took over the role following the removal of his predecessor, who had been retired for this debacle. Syman's solution was to dig a moat twenty feet deep and ten feet wide into the ground and line it with sharpened stakes. It made the far end of the arena look oddly similar to an armed camp but considering the lack of alternatives it was approved and, indeed, achieved satisfactory results.

The arena master's role in a provincial circus is as a jack-of-all-trades and Syman has to balance the several civic functions which his office must serve, rather than concentrating purely upon martial entertainment. The arena is regularly used for public meetings, when the council of elders wish to conduct an open session and it also doubles up as a law court for the occasional trials which are deemed important enough to actually publicise.

Furthermore, fighting is not the only form of entertainment which the arena hosts. Various wandering troupes of performers arc allowcd to ply their trade when no other events hold sway and the athletics competitions which the locals so adore are also held within the stadium. Another form of public entertainment accommodated is rather less aesthetic but none the less highly popular - the execution of criminals. It is Syman's responsibility to act as the local prison warden on top of his other duties, using the holding cells to gather together enough victims to make a mass execution worth turning up for. These have slowly become art-forms in themselves and Syman has responded admirably with various forms of dismissal, from the ever-popular burning at the stake to grand meals for the

local wildlife. One particularly impressive show involved a mass starvation of one hundred and three prisoners who were chained to posts embedded in the ground and simply left there. Each day crowds were allowed in to see who had died, and the final survivor was eventually given his freedom after sixteen days.

In such limited circumstances, Syman is compelled to restrict the nature of the gladiatorial games that he supervises. With only one entrance in the barracks block, little in the way of flashy run outs can be arranged, meaning that some of the combatants must be in the arena ahead of the match. Similarly, the holding pens do not allow wild creatures to be unleashed whilst still inside, although Syman has cunningly got around this by positioning a mobile cage in the arena which can be covered by concealing drapery until it is needed. When the covering is pulled back, the crowds are treated to the sight of whatever beast Syman has managed to acquire for their pleasure.

CITY ARENAS

Only the best get to perform in the large cities, for these are the only places that can support such specialised arenas. Here there is no need to tolerate a weekly flea market or move aside because the auditorium is required by the civic authorities. These structures are owned by the state, although not necessarily directly by the ruler, and they are designed with two specific intentions. Firstly, to provide the citizens of the city, and indeed the whole land, with a focal point for their entertainment and secondly, as a statement of power and grandeur. The various human nations constantly strive to

Hefting his light crossbow across his shoulder, Hjeraldo marched arrogantly into the arena. His was the last bout of the day, and the last bout was always a special one. At the conclusion of a brutal day's combat, the gladiatorial stable reckoned to have been the most successful that day are by the laws of the arena was allowed to nominate a unique match. Any takers then came forward. It was not every day that such a call was answered, and as often as not the crowd were expecting the worst. This day however, they were not disappointed.

It was to be crossbows and short swords. And little else. Still, that didn't matter in the slightest to Hjeraldo, who, as he awaited his opponent, knew that he made a splendid sight, particularly for the noble ladies in the crowd, with whom he soon expected to be a firm favourite. His stable master, Kai Pistorius, had been saving him especially for such a fight as this, and Hjeraldo had absolutely no intention of missing the opportunity. The day had not gone well for the famous stable master and two of his new troupe of gladiators were now dire wolf meat in the catacombs below. Pistorius wanted a victory, and the last one of the day was oft the best remembered. If this went well, Hjeraldo knew he'd have the choice of a dozen noble beds within the week, and Pistorius was legendary for the manner in which he favoured those fighters who had pleased him.

maintain the finest arena, seeing it as a slight to be left behind, the implication being the country is unable to compete in the world. To visiting dwarf and elf dignitaries, these hippodromes are both perturbing and nauseating. They symbolise all that is base in humanity. Even the names of the arenas epitomise, to the likes of elves at least, a low vulgarity, although to humans the title of the arena is as important as its location.

THE DRAGON'S MAW

This arena is typical of what might be found in a large city of any human nation. Constructed within the city walls at the junction of two major thoroughfares, it dominates the skyline with its awesome presence, a symbol of the power of nobility.

The Dragon's Maw took over ten years to construct with a workforce of twenty thousand goblins, prisoners of a highly successful military campaign. The travertine used to face the edifice emptied a whole quarry some thirteen miles from the city, and a double line of goblinoids stretched the entire distance, transferring the stone by hand. Few survived, although this was of little relevance to the humans who would bring their families out specially to watch the humanoid chain labour throughout all seasons.

The arena itself is a huge oval, as is traditional, measuring just under two thousand feet around the outside walls, and its three tiers reach one hundred and fifty feet into the sky. Protruding from the very top tier are wooden poles, designed to take an enormous canvas sun canopy which can be deployed in high summer to protect the spectators from the ravages of the midday sun. Over fifty thousand onlookers can be seated in moderate comfort under this canopy. The arena floor is of wooden construction, covered with a thick layer of sand as is expected.

Invisible beneath the arena, lie the warren of rooms, tunnels and lifts which are really the heart of the stadium. There is room for nearly two thousand gladiators and one thousand beasts, both kept in a sumptuous comfort that would embarrass the landlords of many fine overnight roadhouses. No expense has been spared and on many occasions members of the nobility come down to share meals with a stable of gladiators or to admire a particular creature. One special area is set aside

for the school of gladiators permanently based at the arena. The Dragon's Teeth, as they are known, are considered the best of the best, the pinnacle of gladiatorial vigour, and only one step away from freedom and riches. They wear specially designed armour, evoking the imagery of dragons, and their shields bear draconic motifs. A number of the Dragon's Teeth have survived to attain their freedom and live in the lap of luxury. For each of these though, a thousand others have stained the sands of the arena with their own blood. Such is the price of success.

Access to the arena is through four vast, open archways at ground level, designed like the mouths of dragons, through which the public walk. Three are for the general population but the fourth is restricted to the elite of society and to the gladiators themselves. On games days, only the nobility enter, the gladiators themselves being safely ensconced below. However, when not needed within the arena, the gladiators have upward access by means of a ramp leading up to the gateway. From there they go to various training establishments or, on occasion, into the city itself.

Seating within the arena is, like everywhere else, based upon social rank with the lowermost seated in the highest tier, and the foundation reserved for the aristocracy. Within the lower tier, a large covered podium rises up and back partially into the second section and here royalty and their personal guests are seated. The design of the podium is relatively open, as kings and queens show their subjects just what kind of grandeur their rulers command. At the rear of the podium is a private lift that allows direct access to the subterranean layer below. This has been designed both as a means of viewing the stars of the arena, but also as a potential escape route in the event of unforeseen calamity.

In front of the lower tier, rising nearly three feet above their ground level, a fifteen foot deep bulwark separates the crowd from the arena itself, and if that is not enough, a deep, water-filled trench four feet wide makes sure that the gladiators gain no access to their betters. In fact, it is the contents of the trench rather than the water itself which accomplishes this feat, for within the murky waters reside all manner of carnivorous river life, waiting hopefully for a misplaced foot or falling body.

In the city, gladiatorial spectacles are free. For the upper classes, their limited numbers guarantees a right of access but for the masses, a lottery system determines who will gain the right to see a particular day's sport. Being as games invariably last a number of days, this means a fair proportion of the public have the chance to see the entertainment. It is considered crucial to the continued harmony of the city that the people continue to receive their entertainment free of charge. The spectacles are held at fixed intervals throughout the year, over specific religious holidays and often senior clerics are called to give their blessing to the bloodshed and executions.

Like their country cousins in the provinces, captured criminals are also held over to meet their fate in front of the public. However, in the city, style is as important as content and visiting country folk lucky enough to draw a seat in the upper tiers are often amazed by the imagination of the displays put on for their benefit. On one occasion, Kalaji, an infamous mass poisoner was individually executed in one of the morning prequels to the actual afternoon combats. Rather than simply burn him at the stake

She stood in the entrance to the arena, every nerve as taught as a bowstring. The elves flanked her, chains linking her wrists to theirs. The pair reminded her of frightened children though she was not sure whether the impression was caused by their slight builds or the look of awe-struck fear perfectly mirrored on their faces.

She had no time to prepare them for what they were about to experience. On the other side of the massive gate waited well-armed, well-trained fighters intent on killing anything that stepped through the portal. She took a deep breath and closed her eyes, mind racing to form a plan that would keep her alive long enough to get a decent weapon. At least her feet were not chained.

Just as the trio stepped onto the Sands, she felt the chains at her wrists go slack, the manacles swinging empty by her knees. The elven twins bolted in opposite directions into the arena as she let out an elated battle cry and gripped the heavy chains in either fist, swinging them in fast arcs to get the feel of their weight. Today was going to be a very good day to die. . . for someone else.

or decapitate him, a 'hunt' was arranged, with trees and bushes dotted about the arena, including a number of theoretical hiding places. When the time was right, Kalaji rose from below on one of the lifts simultaneously with two huge tigers on the opposite side of the arena. The beasts had been starved for three days beforehand and were ready to eat anything. The tigers themselves needed separating more than once with whips but once they got the scent of the prisoner, there was much entertainment as he looked for a place of safety, having been told that if he survived for twenty minutes he could walk free. Spying the tallest tree in the arena, Kalaji naturally climbed it, hoping that the hourglass would run its course before the tigers got to him. However, the tree was a carefully constructed trap, positioned on one of the lift trapdoors. With time running out and the circling tigers apparently frustrated, the trapdoor swung up almost imperceptibly, unbalancing the terrified killer and dropping him to his fate.

Whenever games are due to take place, the population of the city swells considerably in size. The rich desert their country estates and the peasants their flocks, and a camp of tents surrounds the already over-sized settlement. Those lucky enough to gain entrance will see almost every type of gladiatorial contest known to man.

GRAND ARENAS

City arenas are deemed by many as the near pinnacle of gladiatorial combat but far above them stand the grand arenas. Such incredible edifices are not meant to be challenged by any rival. The grand arenas are invariably colossal in every sense, dominating the skyline for miles around. They are very much an extension of the ego of the founder,

designed as much to be a monument to him as a place of entertainment for others.

THE HYPOGEUM OF TRALLIOS

Although born in a country with a limited interest in blood sports, from childhood the future King Trallios had been fascinated by the idea of the sands of death. This mostly came about from his education. His father's grip on the throne was by no means secure and for his own safety the young Trallios was sent abroad to be schooled. The land where he was instructed was very different to his home for it was a virile, martial land where gladiatorial combat was much admired and followed. Trallios spent much of his spare time watching and congregating with the gladiators themselves. Despite such inappropriateness, he also began instruction in the gladiatorial arts and in the process became hugely smitten with a gladiator named Jamuga. Needless to say such an affiliation could not be kept silent indefinitely and word eventually got back to Trallios' father, who, still struggling to maintain his own position, could have done well without the scandal of a delinquent teenage heir. One day on his arrival at the arena, Trallios found his entry barred and worse, he saw that Jamuga was rostered to fight Sparg, an Ogre of terrifying repute. The conclusion proved to be foregone.

Initially heartbroken, Trallios continued his studies impassively, nurturing a deep hatred for his own class, seeing them and in particular his father, as responsible for the death of his paramour. He began planning a great and destructive revenge. However, before this could happen, his father was murdered and his homeland thrown into turmoil. Aged only twenty, Trallios was obliged to return to his

kingdom to wrest control from the rebels who had assassinated his father. It did not occur to Trallios this was the end he had planned himself. In fact, he was greatly annoyed that he'd had his designs thwarted. With a large force of mercenaries brought from his adopted land, Trallios returned with a ruthlessness his home had not seen in several generations. Giving no quarter, he crushed his enemies with an efficiency built out of his gladiatorial mindset. After the final victory, he discovered that he had thousands of prisoners, including the clique of rebel generals, and instead of simply executing them on the field an idea began to formulate. Why not treat his conquering soldiers to a victory games?

The prisoners were made to fight to the death in Trallios' camp, the survivors buried alive to teach his subjects once and for all the meaning of rebellion. After the butchery had ended, Trallios felt a vacuum within himself he quickly identified. His own capital had no arena of its own and this he intended to remedy. This would be no ordinary arena though. Trallios had inherited a vast fortune, made greater by the fortunes he seized from the estates of his defeated enemies. The process of creating a unique arena soon began. Trallios scoured the world for the greatest designers, offering small fortunes for the best ideas. He knew himself what the external appearance would be. The royal tombs of his land were tall, stepped pyramids, built with the mathematical precision for which his land was justly famous. Trallios felt nothing but contempt for such intellectualities but he fully intended to use them for his own ends. Knowing the shape of the exterior, Trallios needed the design of the interior itself before he could finalise the concept. The answer came from one of his own court architects - an irony, considering the expense incurred bringing the greatest designers available to his palace. Karthus, a great lover of the theatre, came up with a notion which would appease the sophisticated populous whilst at the same time giving Trallios' new ideas full vent. The king himself could not have given a fig less for his own population's desires but the design was so unique he immediately approved it.

Karthus' idea was as simple as it was ingenious. He would construct the arena in two halves, mounted back to back on a pivot. Partitions were built to block the sound between what Karthus intended to be two gigantic theatrical stages, able to put on the greatest plays and performances simultaneously.

Then, by simply swivelling on the pivot, the whole thing would become a vast gladiatorial arena, with the stages and partitions easily removed. The whole construction, made of wood, would take three years to complete. Seeing the design, one of Karthus' rivals indignantly pointed out that the whole thing looked like two ships on pivots. The insult was a weak one but the notion it put into Trallios' head, after he'd had the reproaching architect beheaded, did not dissipate. The whole arena could possibly be flooded so as to stage mock naval battles, the likes of which Trallios' had heard of, but never personally seen. Karthus, remembering his decapitated colleague, decided this vague idea should be taken seriously.

On the outskirts of the capital was a small, almost circular lake, and Karthus drew up plans to build the whole arena over the lake, turning it into an underground reservoir. He pointed out that such a foundation would be inherently unstable but Trallios seemed wholly unperturbed, brushing away concerns with a wave of a regal hand. He would see to these problems, the king assured Karthus. The same reply came when Karthus pointed out that the extravagant exterior would take twenty years, even with willing labour. He, Trallios, would see to it.

What none knew was that following his devastation at the perceived murder of Jamuga, the future king had turned to dark gods of far off nations, rejecting all the beliefs of his homeland. Maleficent magicks would enable him to construct his dream and in a fraction of the time human hands would take. He installed a number of flagitious wizards in his palace, which steadily became more of a temple dedicated to evil. Rumours of such bestiality reached the ears of the public but there was little they could do. With the revolt crushed, a large force of the mercenaries guarded Trallios. There was no standing army and no sign of his vast wealth running out. The people remained silent, keen neither to experience a second revolt nor the wrath of their monarch.

Trallios realised the need not to overly antagonise his population, whom he hoped to draw into his own depredations en masse, so he allowed Karthus' human workers to complete the interior arena design in the three years allowed. When it was complete, Trallios had the dimensions he needed for his open-topped pyramid. It would ensconce the whole construction, leaving it open to the seasons and inside, row after row of wooden benches would

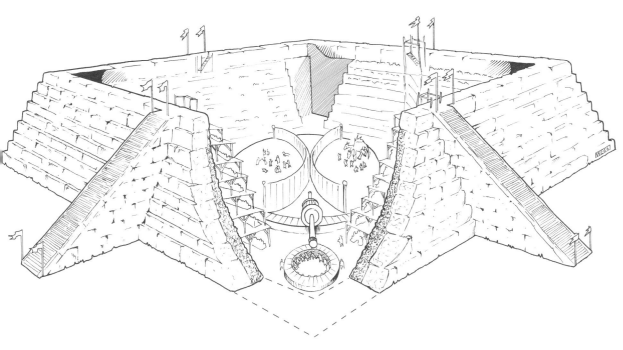

angle down towards the arena. Entrances were planned at the base and half way up the sides, with flights of stairs allowing travel. The interior of the pyramid was a platform of earth and rubble, with an outer shell of stone, painted the traditional amaranth that marked the kings' tombs.

The nine stepped levels each provided standing room for armed guards and inside the walls, between one of the sides and the spectators' benches, Trallios ordered a crypt to be built. On top of the tomb a five-ton slab of stone was rested, held up by massive wooden pegs, awaiting the occupant whose likeness was already mysteriously engraved on the top. It was his intention that when death finally came for him, he would be buried inside his arena and the top enclosed, entombing him with the spirits of his beloved gladiators. Only Karthus and his construction team were aware of this plan, and only Karthus' life was spared on its completion.

During the days that followed, the human and monstrous workers earmarked for the project did their work but at night, away from prying eyes, the demons to whom Trallios had aligned himself continued, working at an inhuman speed to see the great pyramid completed in two years instead of the expected twenty. All knew that fell magic was behind such an unearthly accomplishment, yet none dared question it. After all, it was reasoned, now that Trallios' will was assuaged, would life not go back to normality, and with a splendid arena no less?

In essence the people were right. The inaugural festival of games lasted forty days and saw every form of spectacle known to man. Trallios inducted his people into the thrill of the games, starting with chariot races, then gladiatorial combats, and ending in the flooding of the whole arena to allow a gigantic naval battle involving a dozen ships and five thousand sailors. By the end, the sands of death had been ingrained onto the hearts of his people, and they clamoured for more. Trallios obliged, and soon his great Hypogeum became famed throughout the world.

Because of the nature of the design, no subterranean tunnel system, common in city arenas, was possible. Accordingly all the contestants, human and otherwise, had to be brought into the arena from the massive encampment which sprung up outside. At first constructed of wood, these buildings quickly evolved into stone as it was realised the installation would be permanent. The Hypogeum and its surrounding buildings became almost a town unto themselves and before long the whole complex was closed off by a tall palisade patrolled by Trallios' taciturn guards. Entry, other than on specific games days was strictly limited and the king seemingly spent more time amongst the swelling buildings of this conurbation than he did in his own palace. Rumours of evil goings on and numinous sounds ensured that the patrolling guards got little in the way of disturbance.

THE ARENAS

By day, however, Trallios immersed himself fully in the sands of death. Feeling only contempt for human life, he wanted nothing more than to be revered as the genius behind the games. He spent hours coming up with new and original concepts and in this he ironically gained the favour of his own people who, as the years passed, came to relish the games as much as did their king. Rarely did the split stages get used for anything as mundane as a play and Karthus looked on dejectedly as the crowds were entertained by a 'hunt' on one side whilst matched pairs duelled on the other. This was not what he had had in mind at all.

Trallios rarely saw his old architect though and when he did, he certainly would not have taken any notice of the fellow's feelings. Trallios lived for one man, and that man was Trallios. He had reached forty without taking a wife, preferring to spend time with his gladiators. On occasion he would even fight in the arena himself, though it was widely believed none would dare harm the king, and his well-choreographed bouts always ended in victory. He even took to fighting various beasts and creatures, alone or with groups of his favourite fighters, although it was made certain in advance the victim was suitably impaired by the administration of debilitating drugs or slow poisons. He was not, after all, a fool.

That Trallios had been able to corrupt the core of an entire nation within the space of a single generation spoke poorly of the veneer of civilisation they had considered so firm. However, he was not able to bend them completely to his will, and with the new-found love of the games came an aesthetic nature which meant the vanquished always stood a good chance of survival, much to Trallios' annoyance. He always liked to see the loser slain but, even seated in his golden chair on the royal rostrum, he felt obliged to adhere to the majority verdict. It was the tradition, after all.

Trallios, having an organisational mind, demanded the same of his games. He introduced a standard opening ceremony whence the gladiators, on entering, completed a full circuit of the arena before halting in front of the royal dais. There they bowed in greeting before opening their arms in salute. An official

would then inspect the weapons and confirm to the king all was in order. On special occasions, the king would come down from the rostrum himself to do the honours or if he was fighting, then he would graciously allow the official to examine him as well, much to the crowd's pleasure.

With the precautions he took and the protective magicks with which he was constantly surrounded, Trallios lived well into his sixties before fate overtook him. Seeing his once virile body beginning to deteriorate, Trallios enquired of his demonologists what might be done to alleviate his death. Recklessly it was decided he should be possessed with a great demon, to enhance his life indefinitely. The idea appealed to Trallios and preparations quickly began for the ceremony. The building in question was one of those near the Hypogeum to which only a few had access, and it took all of his demonologists gathered together to call the demon from the infernal planes. Had they not erred with the demon's true name, the gods alone know what the result might have been. As it was, the creature arrived and took the opportunity to slay all those who had falsely called upon it. It then took possession of Trallios, drinking his thoughts and torturing his body, mind and soul.

They found his mutilated remains in the centre of the arena, the sands of death never having been so aptly named. Only his head was intact, perversely left to

28

show all whom it had been. Of the killer, there was no trace. The same day, the bloodbath in the nearby idolatry was found and so appalling was the sight that the building was deemed irrecoverable and destroyed. So perished Trallios, the last of his line.

Yet he left an endowment to his people. Whilst they retained their aesthetic character, they were also unable to relinquish the games to which they had become habituated. A ruling council of nobles replaced the monarchy and the games continued as before, but in such a manner that the Hypogeum became the very kernel of the nation. Famed throughout the world, any aficionado of the arena aims to visit the Hypogeum at least once.

The screeching of the iron portcullis at the opposite end of the arena marked the impending arrival of his opponent, and the young gladiator's confidence faltered for a second when he saw the heavy crossbow carried so comfortably by the human female. With his weakness for women, it was lucky that she looked like the far end of a troll. At least there would be no distractions.

It did mean a change of plans though. He had to assume that she knew what she was doing, which meant he was outmatched in terms of power. Likely he'd go down before she would, and that wouldn't do at all. However, martial skills were not the only talents that Pistorius drilled into his gladiators. He believed in psychology, and he hammered it into his fighters that a quick mind was as important as any steel. Now he'd see.

He began to laugh. Loudly.

The female gladiator looked up suddenly in surprise. She had been adjusting the tension on her own crossbow, awaiting the trumpet call to action. Now, a mere hundred feet away, this oiled buffoon was laughing. Laughing at her. Rage began to burn inside her. Cireel, for that was her name, searched her dull mind for a response, but none was forthcoming. The School of Amazons had not trained her for such an occurrence. Now, even the crowd was silenced, stunned by her opponent who seemed to be collapsing in paroxysms of laughter – at her expense!

Hjeraldo surreptitiously glanced at his opponent as he continued his fakery. He could practically see the fumes escaping her head. One more push should do it.

'By all the gods! She has the face of jackal and the body of a baboon!' he shouted to the crowd. As one they burst into fits of laughter themselves. It was too much for Cireel. She dropped the still-loaded crossbow, drew her short sword and charged across the arena.

She saw the bolt with her right eye alone. It was buried in her left eye and had lodged up to the shaft. As she collapsed onto the sands, Cireel saw her vanquisher had already turned and was recieving the adulation of the crowd.

THE GLADIATOR CAMPAIGN

This sourcebook provides a wealth of information dedicated to Games Masters for integrating arenas and gladiatorial combat into their campaign worlds. The five example arenas provided on p14 are sufficiently detailed to be dropped into any suitable town or city with the bare minimum of effort on the part of the Games Master and whilst the construction of a grand arena may have a powerful impact upon the city it dominates, sufficient information is given on easing the transition. Players themselves will readily adopt the new weapons and feats even if they never set foot within an arena themselves and many may just be dying for an excuse to purchase and use one of the chariots on p53.

There are two principle ways in which arenas may be introduced into an existing campaign world – as scenario hooks and plot devices in regular adventures, or as a full-bodied gladiator campaign. In this chapter, we will take a look at both.

THE REGULAR CAMPAIGN

The standard dungeoneering party of clerics, rangers, wizards and the rest may happen across an arena in any city they visit – or even whilst adventuring under the earth, as exemplified by the orcish arena on p17. Such arenas are best introduced when the party visits such a settlement for the very first time as then they can explore the social dynamics of an arena and its effect upon a culture as outsiders, not needing the benefit of the information within this sourcebook immediately, but discovering it as required.

Such a party is likely to, initially at least, stay on the outskirts of the arena and its many characters. They may be hired by stable masters to cause trouble for rivals, or by someone distressed at the enslavement of a family member who is due to be thrust into the arena with no training. Paladins and lawful good-aligned clerics may have a serious problem with a society that enslaves part of its population to provide lethal entertainment, though they had better be of high level if they seek to do anything about such concerns. The nobles, arena managers and stable masters will be loathed to suffer any interruption to their profitable status quo.

S.Purdy2001

As the party sinks further into the callous and cynical society surrounding any arena, they will begin to learn of the relationships between those who run the games and, players being what they are, will inevitably run afoul of many powerful people, whether intentionally or not. This will occur even if they do no more than accept straight offers of employment. By aiding one stable master, they will irritate his rivals. By taking an arena manager as a patron, they will possibly gain the enmity of all the stable masters. If they perform any arena-related tasks for an ambitious noble, they are set to become wanted men by almost everyone else involved in the running of the arena. From this initial starting point, they may well be captured and enslaved by the enemies they make. Such parties are, of course, best disposed of within the arena itself, leading to a full-bodied gladiator campaign as detailed later. Alternatively, quick-witted parties may succeed in confounding the enemies they create. Those who choose not to leave the city in short order may begin to fully embrace the world of the arena, either stepping on to the sands of death as freemen or setting up their own expensive but highly profitable stable. If this is achieved, you can be sure that many established stable masters will take nefarious action against any newcomers who threaten to upset their delicate balance of politics and profit.

When it comes to player characters running their own stable, you might like to consider using the Sands of Death game on p64 as a basic framework with which to structure the running of a stable. The only word of caution is to always remember you are running a role-playing game, whereas Sands of Death does nothing more than portray games days in an abstract fashion. Always be ready to disregard the rules presented in Sands of Death in the interests of both your main story line and keeping the players off-balance and unsure of quite what will happen next. In between these games days, keep the players busy with rival stable masters, awesome gladiators in other stables and corrupt arena managers. Such scenarios may or may not hold the players' enjoyment for a great length of time, but they will certainly be good for a few gaming sessions.

SCENARIO HOOKS AND IDEAS

Below are presented just a few initial ideas for adventures with which draw a regular adventuring party into the world of arena combat and entertainment.

† Captured by orcs, the players are forced to fight for their freedom in the arena on p17.

† A tearful young girl begs the party to free her father who has been enslaved and is set to fight in the arena the next day (note: young girls are always well-used in this fashion – make them older or male and most players will expect payment).

† Caught red-handed in the midst of some crime, the players are quickly sent to a stable master desperate to provide gladiators for tomorrow's battle.

† Enjoying a quiet drink in a favoured tavern after vanquishing a marauding hobgoblin tribe, the players are approached by a weasel-faced man promising good pay if only they cause a gladiator, who has been annoying his own employer with continued victories, to disappear. Permanently. With extreme prejudice.

† A rather harried-looking arena manager puts a general call out to adventurers prepared to procure rare and dangerous creatures such as carrion crawlers, hydras and trolls. Rival adventuring parties may also be interested in the large rewards, however, and could seek to intimidate or remove rivals.

† The local thieves' guild has been taking a keen interest in the arena of late, fixing games and silencing troublesome stable masters. The players get mixed up in these machinations and are encouraged to sell themselves into slavery as gladiators to get to the heart of the plot.

THE GLADIATOR CAMPAIGN

A full-blown gladiator campaign will involve all the player characters becoming enslaved or, more likely, have them start in servitude, forced to fight every games day in the arena. Such a campaign may well not last for years of playing time but it can certainly provide many sessions of tense action and easily serve as the foundation for a more regular campaign – by the time the party has survived many matches within the arena, they will be truly awesome warriors, capable of tackling any evil in the world once freedom is gained.

'Rosanellwyia and Gildena.' Two sets of dark eyes peered at her expectantly.

She made a face. Her mouth seemed to refuse to properly pronounce the elves names though they had repeated them a thousand times. 'I will call you Rose and Gilda. You will call me Hamli. Short names are better used on the sands. I'll not have my hair trimmed at the neck for trying to remember how to pronounce your names.'

Hamli winced as the healer dabbed salve on her shoulder. 'I overheard the stable master. We're slated for a battle tomorrow. If we work together, we'll live to see the sun set. Act scared. Run, scream, pretend to swoon, then stab them in the back or just under the ribs while they're gloating and posing for the crowd. Use their ego against them.'

'And will you scream and run?' Rose tilted her head questioningly.

Hamli smiled. 'Yes. . . directly at the centre of their lines. The contrast should confuse them long enough to take out a good portion of them before they understand what is happening.'

Rose and Gilda looked at each other then back to the human. 'We think perhaps you are not so much a barbarian as they seem to believe.'

In a gladiator campaign, the initial choices for characters will likely be very restrictive compared to what they are normally used to. After all, the action takes place in the arena, so characters had better be able to fight well! This is, in itself, no bad thing. Focussed campaigns of this nature are relatively easy for a Games Master to write and players with immediately defined goals are generally happier than those left to wander aimlessly.

We would recommend that starting characters are limited to fighters, barbarians, rogues and monks. Spellcasters, even clerics and druids, are likely to be made to suffer for their special powers where they may be better off concentrating on pure combat abilities. There need be no restrictions on race but players wishing to take halflings and gnomes should be warned how tough life is likely to be for them. However, we would also direct Games Masters to review the possibility of starting all player characters off with the slave NPC class on p35. Players resistant to the idea may well be swayed with the Born to Fight class feature and in any case, they have a free choice to multiclass as something else as soon as they hit second level. The use of the slave class can really hammer home to the players the position their characters are in and make for a truly memorable campaign. After all, imagine a great barbarian king, holding dominion over an entire nation. Though a 20th level killing machine now, he began his life as a slave before entering the arena. Sound familiar? Think you can persuade your players to accept the slave class now? I knew you could.

BREAKING THE SHACKLES

The ultimate goal for the gladiator campaign has to be the gaining of freedom, the escape from slavery. Until that is achieved, players will always be ultimately subject to the whim of others and whilst they may become incredibly skilled gladiators and fulfil various plans and ambitions

in the meantime, their destiny will never be truly theirs. This can take one of two forms – at relatively low levels, they may simply gain the opportunity to escape and begin new lives by running far from the arena. Alternatively, they may become true celebrities on the sands of death and get into the position of either leading a massed slave revolt or directly challenging the position of a jealous city ruler who would just as soon see them dead. Again, I am sure this is all fairly familiar.

The trick in directing such a campaign is to forever put obstacles in the way of your players until you are ready to release them into the rest of the world. Rivalries between other gladiators and stables are obvious plot devices and the attentions of an interested and powerful noble are always likely to provide a great deal of trouble for the players, whether he wants to help or hinder their careers. Gladiators with a high Fame score will quickly find their celebrity status brings its own problems as they

c©rteReal

become a prime target for opponents, rivals, assassins and those wishing to profit from either their victory or defeat.

ETERNAL COMBAT

One of the first criticisms levelled at gladiator campaigns is that, surely, it revolves around pure combat. Well, maybe not. You need only have, say, one match per gaming session and the fact that the more elaborate matches, such as Lord of the Pyramid, can provide over an hour of fast, intense gaming time makes this kind of campaign very attractive to a Games Master with limited time to prepare for adventures.

Outside of the arena though, players can be given more than enough to occupy their time, even whilst enslaved. Established gladiators in a stable are likely to take a dim view to newcomers who cover themselves in glory. Once they become the top dogs of the stable, gladiators with other masters are going to begin taking an interest in the players. Rivalries are an important plot device to introduce early on – have a gladiator give a player a real kicking in the arena and yet spare him when mercy is asked for. That should be enough for the NPC to earn the enmity of most players. Scenarios can also arise through the shadier dealings of the players' stable master and the arena manager, and they may find initially fair odds stacked heavily against them within the arena if plans and deals begin to go awry.

At the end of the day, such people as Stanley Kubrick, Ridley Scott and Dino de Laurentiis have made popular, indeed block-busting, movies based on gladiators. There need be nothing boring or monotonous in such a focussed campaign and you have the works of these great directors to provide readily accessible source material. Try out a gladiator campaign, even if only as the base for more regular adventuring – your players will thank you for it.

Part II
Gladiatorial Combat

Characters of the Arena

Slave

The practice of slavery has been outlawed in the majority of truly civilised nations but there are still many slavers who operate covertly in the shadowy underworld or by the leave of corrupt lawmakers. However, the presence of a large gladiatorial arena often necessitates the use of slaves to supply a continuous source of combatants for the sands. In such towns and cities, slavery is deemed a part of everyday life, the removal of freedom from another sentient being taken for granted. Indeed, one may measure wealth and status simply through the number of slaves owned and outside of the blood-stained arena, a slave's life may be deemed safe, if monotonous. Despite common perceptions amongst freemen from other nations, slaves are rarely treated poorly as they are just too expensive for their owners to discard carelessly.

The slave is an NPC character class. Player characters may start as slaves and this can make for an exciting start to a campaign as they first work to gain their freedom, then adopt new character classes to continue adventuring.

Hit Die: d6

Class Skills

The slave's class skills (and the key ability for each skill are Climb (Str), Handle Animal (Cha), Jump (Str), Listen (Wis), Spot (Wis), Swim (Str) and Use Rope (Dex). See Core Rulebook I for skill descriptions.

Skill points at 1st level: (2+Int modifier) x 4.
Skill points at each additional level: 2 + Int modifier.

Class Features

The following are the class features of the slave NPC class.

Weapon and Armour Proficiency: The slave is proficient with one simple weapon. He is not proficient with weapons, armour or shields. Note that armour check penalties for armour heavier than leather apply to the skills Balance, Climb, Escape Artist, Hide, Jump, Move Silently, Pick Pocket and Tumble.

Former Life: Slaves may have come from any walk of life before being captured and forced into servitude. A slave character may treat any skill as a cross-class skill during character generation. Such skills chosen at this time remain as cross-class skills throughout the character's life. No others may be added as cross-class skills once a new character level is gained.

Born to Fight: Some gladiators in cities with grand arenas are simply bred to fight. From the

The Slave				
NPC Level	Base Attack Bonus	Fort Save	Ref Save	Will Save
1	+0	+0	+0	+0
2	+1	+0	+0	+0
3	+1	+1	+1	+1
4	+2	+1	+1	+1
5	+2	+1	+1	+1

The text on this page is designated Open Game Content

moment they are born, they are trained as gladiators, their only destiny to someday die upon the sands of death. Such slaves may add a +1 bonus to their Strength, Dexterity or Constitution ability scores, but suffer a –1 penalty to either Intelligence, Wisdom or Charisma. They are also proficient with all simple and martial weapons, light armour and shields.

A New Life: When multiclassing from the slave class, characters never suffer experience penalties. In addition, the slave class does not count towards the total number of classes when calculating such penalties. Once the slave class has been left behind, it is effectively assumed that the character never was a slave.

Starting Gear
The slave starts with no equipment of his own.

GLADIATOR CHAMPION

There are few as famed or renowned in any major city as the gladiator champion. His is the name spoken in taverns by drunks, around the dinner table in noble society and in the streets by the masses. Children can even be seen emulating him. Everyone talks of his latest match in the arena, where he strode forth on to the sands of death to claim yet another victory for his stable master.

Whilst a fearsome warrior in his own right, the gladiator champion has honed his skills and abilities to one end alone – victory within the arena. Sheer slaughter takes second place for this true expert. Specialised in engaging the crowd as well as performing amazing displays of courage and skill, he may seem a little out of place if freedom is ever attained and he starts travelling with a party of adventurers to slay orcs. If the truth be told though, few gladiator champions look forward to possible freedom. Most are hooked upon the roar of the crowd at their entrance, the feeling of thousands of eyes watching their every sword stroke, and the unparalleled feeling of victory when yet another opponent is vanquished to the ecstatic cries of the mob. Whether fighting blind, unarmed, chained or on the back of a speeding chariot, there is no field of combat he cannot hope to excel in. There are none who can truly compete with the experienced gladiator champion whilst on his home ground – the sands of the arena.

Hit Die: d10.

Requirements
To qualify to become a gladiator champion, a character must fulfil all the following criteria.

Base Attack Bonus: +3 or higher
Skills: Handle Animal 6+, Perform 4+
Feats: Fame & Glory

Class Skills
The gladiator champion's class skills (and the key ability for each skill) are Bluff (Cha), Climb (Str), Craft (Int), Handle Animal (Cha), Intimidate (Cha), Jump (Str), Perform (Cha), Ride (Dex), and Tumble (Dex). See Core Rulebook I for skill descriptions.

Skill points at each level: 4 + Int modifier.

Class Features
All of the following are class features of the gladiator champion prestige class.

Weapon and Armour Proficiency: The gladiator champion is proficient in all simple and martial weapons, all armour and shields. Note that armour check penalties for armour heavier than leather apply to the skills Balance, Climb, Escape Artist, Hide, Jump, Move Silently, Pick Pocket and Tumble.

Exotic Weaponry: Starting at 1st level, one exotic weapon proficiency feat is received for every class level attained in gladiator champion. Such a hero of the arena quickly learns to use the far more esoteric weaponry in order to put a better show on for the crowd.

Renown: Starting at 2nd level, the class level in gladiator champion is added to his Fame score every time a new level is attained in this class. Thus, at 2nd level, two points are added to Fame, at 3rd level, three more points will be added, and so on.

Perform Bonus: At 3rd, 6th and 9th levels, the gladiator champion receives a competence bonus on his Perform checks as he learns to control the crowd and display his talents with ever more expertise.

Stable Status: From 4th level onwards, the gladiator champion's fame and notoriety is such that his stable master must divert more of the match winnings to his purse, lest the gladiator champion decide he would rather join another stable. In the Sands of Death game on p64, 40% of the gladiator

The Gladiator Champion

Class Level	Base Attack	Fort Save	Ref Save	Will Save	Special
1	+1	+2	+0	+0	Exotic Weaponry
2	+2	+3	+0	+0	Renown
3	+3	+3	+1	+1	Perform Bonus +2
4	+4	+4	+1	+1	Stable Status
5	+5	+4	+1	+1	Devastating Attack 1d8
6	+6	+5	+2	+2	Perform Bonus +4
7	+7	+5	+2	+2	Lightning Strike
8	+8	+6	+2	+2	Devastating Attack 2d8
9	+9	+6	+3	+3	Perform Bonus +6
10	+10	+7	+3	+3	Improved Death Move

champion's winnings in any match are now added to his purse. In regular campaigns, the Games Master must judge the effect of this class feature for himself, but the gladiator champion should now receive roughly twice the gold he used to earn in the arena.

Devastating Attack: At 5th level, the gladiator champion gains the ability to unleash one mighty, awe-inspiring attack that can easily crush the defences of any opponent. The crowd often goes wild when they see this carefully mastered move and it soon becomes a signature of the gladiator champion when he steps into the arena. A devastating attack may only ever be performed with one type of weapon – the gladiator champion must specify this weapon immediately. A devastating attack must be performed as a full round action. One attack roll is made as normal and if it hits, an extra 1d8 damage will be caused. At 8th level, this damage bonus goes up to 2d8. The devastating attack will not work against creatures who are immune to critical hits.

Lightning Strike: Gained at 7th level, the gladiator champion gains a +2 bonus to his Initiative. This may stack with other bonuses, such as the Improved Initiative feat.

Improved Death Move: At 10th level, the gladiator champion gains the most awesome attack of all – the improved death move. In all respects, this class feature works in the same fashion as the Death Move feat on p40, with the following exceptions. The gladiator champion need not wait for a target to drop to 0 hit points or less to use the improved death move. Instead, the target need only be on 25% or

less of its starting hit points, though it may not be of a size class larger than that of the gladiator champion. Both the gladiator champion and the target make opposed Strength or Dexterity (gladiator champion's choice of which) checks to determine the success of the improved death move. Their respective character level and/or Hit Dice are used as bonus modifiers to this roll. If the gladiator champion beats his target's check with his own, the target is automatically slain in a very grisly manner.

BEAST HANDLER

There are many types of specialised gladiator to be found within the arena but few can excite the crowd as much as the beast handler – not for what he is, or what he can do but for the wild and fantastic creatures he brings with him onto the sands. From wild cats to the huge and truly dangerous manticore and hydra, the beast handler delights the crowd with his charges, getting them to perform amazing tricks that defy imagination, when they are not tearing gladiators to pieces. Such creatures are usually sent into the arena alone to fight but occasionally the beast handler will stand beside his beloved creature, fighting alongside it in a display of devastating teamwork. It is true that it is often the creature that gets the notice of the crowd rather than the beast handler himself but then, few veteran beast handlers truly seem to care.

Hit Die: d10.

Requirements

To qualify to become a beast handler, a character must fulfil all the following criteria.

Base Attack Bonus: +2 or higher
Skills: Handle Animal 4+

Class Skills

The beast handler's class skills (and the key ability for each skill) are Bluff (Cha), Climb (Str), Craft (Int), Handle Animal (Cha), Intimidate (Cha), Jump (Str), Perform (Cha), Ride (Dex), and Tumble (Dex). See Core Rulebook I for skill descriptions.

Skill points at each level: 4 + Int modifier.

Class Features

All of the following are class features of the beast handler prestige class.

Weapon and Armour Proficiency: The beast handler is proficient in all simple and martial weapons, all armour and shields. Note that armour check penalties for armour heavier than leather apply to the skills Balance, Climb, Escape Artist, Hide, Jump, Move Silently, Pick Pocket and Tumble.

Favoured Beast: The beast handler must select one animal or creature – those listed in italics on p65 are good examples of what may be chosen. Once this choice has been made, it may never be changed. After three months of constant training with this creature, the beast handler can influence it far easier than any other. Any Animal Empathy, Handle Animal, or Ride check involving this creature will gain a synergy bonus equal to the beast handler's class level. If the favoured beast is later slain, the beast handler may only replace it after a period of three months continuous training with another creature of the same species.

Loyalty: The favoured beast will always attempt to attack the beast handler's opponents in combat if it is not engaged itself.

Blood Frenzy: If the beast handler is wounded in combat, his favoured beast will gain a +2 circumstance bonus to all attack and damage rolls against whomever wounded him.

Teamwork: When attacking the same target, both the beast handler and his favoured beast gain a +4 flanking bonus instead of the usual +2, such is their teamwork when fighting together.

Improved Training: Through constant training, the favoured beast gains a competence bonus to his attack rolls equal to the beast handler's class level.

Undying Loyalty: So long as the favoured beast is within five feet of the beast handler, it may receive any attack directed at the beast handler himself. This must be declared before the attack roll is actually made but counts as a free action. The attack is then resolved against the favoured beast.

CHARIOTEER

There are few matches that can grab the attention of the crowd so much as the chariot race. Fast, exciting and utterly lethal to the novice gladiator, chariots may be the most deadly devices to enter the arena. Two or more charging horses pulling a lightweight chariot, sporting massive scythes and bearing skilled charioteers are a truly awesome weapon. To those who dare regularly compete in chariot races, the rewards may well outweigh such risks for a successful charioteer will find his career in the arena guaranteed, with the crowd always ready to welcome him with shouts of bloodlust and adulation.

Hit Die: d10.

Requirements

To qualify to become a charioteer, a character must fulfil all the following criteria.

The Beast Handler					
Class Level	Base Attack	Fort Save	Ref Save	Will Save	Special
1	+1	+2	+0	+0	Favoured Beast, Loyalty
2	+2	+3	+0	+0	Blood Frenzy
3	+3	+3	+1	+1	Teamwork
4	+4	+4	+1	+1	Improved Training
5	+5	+4	+1	+1	Undying Loyalty

Class Level	Base Attack	Fort Save	Ref Save	Will Save	Special
					The Charioteer
1	+1	+2	+0	+0	Superb Control +2
2	+2	+3	+0	+0	Survivor, Love of the Crowd
3	+3	+3	+1	+1	Superb Control +4
4	+4	+4	+1	+1	Lethal Sideswipe
5	+5	+4	+1	+1	Superb Control +6

Base Attack Bonus: +5 or higher
Skills: Handle Animal 8+
Fame: 12+

Class Skills

The charioteer's class skills (and the key ability for each skill) are Bluff (Cha), Handle Animal (Cha), Intimidate (Cha), Jump (Str), Perform (Cha), and Ride (Dex). See Core Rulebook I for skill descriptions.

Skill points at each level: 4 + Int modifier.

Class Features

All of the following are class features of the charioteer prestige class.

Weapon and Armour Proficiency: The charioteer is proficient in all simple and martial weapons, all armour and shields. Note that armour check penalties for armour heavier than leather apply to the skills Balance, Climb, Escape Artist, Hide, Jump, Move Silently, Pick Pocket and Tumble.

Superb Control: The charioteer is gifted with a sixth sense that allows him to control his horses and chariot as if they were extensions of his own body. At 1st, 3rd and 5th level, he receives a synergy bonus to all Handle Animal checks when attempting to avoid overturning his chariot.

Survivor: At 2nd level, the charioteer only receives half the normal damage

when his chariot overturns. A successful Reflex check will result in no damage being taken at all.

Love of the Crowd: The charioteer has the flare and vitality all renowned charioteers seem to possess and the crowd eagerly await every appearance. From 2nd level onwards, the charioteer automatically receives 2 points of Fame for every chariot race instead of just 1.

Lethal Sideswipe: Few opponents will willingly draw up alongside the charioteer for the force of his sideswipes are legendary throughout the arena. At 4th level, the charioteer may add his character level as a positive modifier to his Handle Animal check whenever he initiates a sideswipe. This bonus does not apply if an opponent sideswipes him.

GLADIATORIAL FEATS

The debate is endless and rages on in taverns and around the dinner tables of the upper classes. Who is the superior combatant? The noble knight? Or the lowly gladiator? Arguments are put forward and dismissed after much speculation. Surely the knight is the greater fighter, for he must battle against a wide range of man and beast, for causes great and honoured, in defence of his nation. No, no, comes the retort – a gladiator fights just as wide a range of enemies and yet must do so whilst constantly handicapped by someone else's choice of weapon and armour. And furthermore, he does it constantly, each and every day of his life. To the true knight or gladiator, such speculation is pointless to the extreme. Each knows that there is little difference in raw combat, wherever it takes place and however it is fought. You must thrust your weapon into another's flesh before they are able to do it to you. That, at the end of the day, is all that matters. The differences of armour, weapon and even outlook are minor by comparison.

It is recognised, however, that the gladiators of the arena are truly remarkable fighters, far more than the mere entertainers the common man may presume them to be. There are many techniques and ploys that seem to be only learnt through the butchery of the arena and any gladiator who survives for some length of time is going to be in possession of skills that are likely to impress the hardiest of adventuring warriors.

Presented here are a range of feats any character competing in the arena may learn with experience. At the Games Master's option, such feats may also be used throughout regular campaigns by those who meet the listed prerequisites.

Armour Penetration (General)
You are highly skilled at seeking out the weak points in your opponent's armour. The slightest gap between metal plates becomes a target for your weapon, allowing you to penetrate armour with relative ease.

Prerequisites: Base attack bonus +6 or higher
Benefit: You add +1 to your attack roll in melee combat if your opponent is wearing armour. Shields and natural armour may not be negated through the use of Armour Penetration. You bonus to attack cannot exceed the armour class bonus your opponent receives from his armour.

Armour Specialisation (General)
Choose either light, medium or heavy armour. You are especially adept at wearing this category of armour to best effect, instinctively turning to catch each blow on the most solid plates. Sword strikes and spear thrusts will merely bounce or slide off.

Prerequisites: Proficient with armour type, base attack bonus +2 or higher.
Benefit: You add a +1 competence bonus to your Armour Class in melee combat whilst wearing this type of armour.

Chariot Control (General)
You are one of the finest charioteers ever to have graced the arena. The control you exhibit over your vehicle defies rational explanation – you are able to make the tightest turns at high speeds and even the most complicated courses hold little fear for you.

Prerequisites: Handle Animal 8+
Benefit: You may always make tight turns, as described on p53, with no Handle Animal check needed to avoid overturning.

Death Move (General)
You are a master of the arena, one who can both sway the crowd and truly be a dangerous foe to face. After defeating an enemy in the arena, you may perform a special death move you have practised to intimidate other gladiators and cause the crowd to howl. The specifics of the death move are up to you, but actions such as decapitating the head of an enemy, impaling him on a spike or even ripping out his spinal column are particular favourites with the mob.

Prerequisites: Base attack bonus +6 or higher
Benefit: If you make either a Strength or Dexterity check (your choice which) at DC 15, you may perform your death move on an enemy you have reduced to zero or lower hit points. Only melee weapons may be used in a death move. You will automatically gain a temporary +1 morale bonus on attack and damage rolls that will last until the end of the match. You will also gain one permanent point of Fame. In all other respects, this feat is treated as performing a coup de grace, as detailed in Core Rulebook I.

Distract (General)

You are one of the few gladiators who can regularly throw his opponent off-balance and reduce the effectiveness of his attacks. Through a combination of feints and diversions, you can keep an enemy on his toes and yet retain your own devastating attacks.

Prerequisites: Charisma 13+
Benefit: The use of this feat is a free action. If you can succeed a Charisma check at DC 10 + your opponent's character level/Hit Dice, you will cause him to take only partial actions in the next round of combat. This will only work on opponents who have an Intelligence score of at least 3, as animals and other base creatures will simply ignore your feints and fancy moves as they seek to rend you apart.

Fame & Glory (General)

All veteran gladiators understand the benefits of having the crowd on their side. Indeed, many gladiators actively seek the recognition and have a very basic need to hear the roar of support from thousands of spectators each and every time they walk on to the sands of death. To keep the memory of their fights fresh in the minds of the crowd, gladiators often adopt showman-like rituals, performing comic dances, amazing feats of skill with their weapons or even encouraging the mob to join in with favoured chants. You are a master at such ploys and the crowd is always guaranteed to remember your name and greet you whenever you walk into the arena.

Prerequisites: Fame 10+
Benefit: You immediately gain a permanent +10 bonus to your Fame score.

Fearsome Display (General)

You know your weapons intimately and can readily spin through a series of rapid manoeuvres, twirling blades and making a weapon sing as it slices through the air. By performing such quick and lethal looking movers, you can intimidate your opponent before a blow is struck.

Prerequisites: Base attack bonus +3 or higher, Intimidate rank 6 or higher
Benefit: You may select one opponent within 30 feet to perform the fearsome display to. Make an Intimidate check at DC 10 + opponent's character level. Only melee weapons may be used in a fearsome display. Your opponent will automatically gain a temporary –1 morale penalty on attack and damage rolls that will last to the end of the match. You will also gain one permanent point of Fame. This feat may only be used against an opponent once per combat.

Improved Chariot Sideswipe (General)

Other charioteers fear you when you enter the arena, for your skill at controlling your vehicle is legendary. Few will willingly race side by side with your thundering chariot, for your ability to destroy an opponent with the most casual of sideswipes is terrible to behold.

Prerequisites: Chariot Control
Benefit: You gain a +6 competence bonus on all Handle Animal checks you make when performing a sideswipe with your chariot.

Taunt (General)

Gladiators always goad one another in the arena, making various references to their parentage and fighting ability, or lack of. You, however, have developed this into a fine art, whereby even the most disciplined gladiator may be encouraged to drop his guard and launch a poorly thought attack out of sheer anger. An enraged enemy will be far less accurate in his attacks but if he ever connects, is likely to do far more damage.

Prerequisites: None
Benefit: Performing a taunt is a free action but may only be used on enemies with an Intelligence score of 3 or higher. Make an opposing Will check between yourself and one of the enemies you are fighting in melee combat. If you win, your opponent responds to the taunt (feel free to specify exactly the nature of your goading – reminding another gladiator of poor previous performance or the size of his weapon are always good starting points). Your opponent's next attack will suffer a –2 penalty to the attack roll but also a +1 bonus to any damage roll. Taunts may be performed against one opponent each round. Both yourself and your opponent must speak and understand the same language for this feat to have any effect, though this is not usually a problem within an arena.

TYPES OF MATCHES

As well an ensuring the smooth running of the arena and the stable masters, it is the responsibility of the arena manager to provide the greatest entertainment for the people, to grant a spectacle guaranteed to live on in memory. All manner of diversions and events are planned, from pre-match performers to trained animals capable of astounding tricks. All this, however, revolves around the main attractions – the gladiators who walk onto the sands of death to fight for the pleasure of the crowd, all the while knowing it may be their last combat.

The crowd are both cynical and jaded though and an arena manager must be a creative individual with few scruples, as well as a consummate showman forever seeking newer and deadlier challenges for the gladiators. Throughout a day's games, matches will become ever more elaborate and trying, each a spectacle better than the one before, building up to a grand finale that sates the blood thirst of the crowd until the next day.

Presented here are just a few examples of the types of matches the crowd can expect to see in any one day. The Games Master is encouraged to devise new and interesting matches for his players, be they mere spectators or actual gladiators. Each type of match is described along with details governing initial set up and any special rules to be applied. If a match is listed as having random weapons and armour, a Games Master should select suitable weaponry for the gladiators participating in the combat. Alternatively, the table on p67 may be used to generate random arms and armour. Unless otherwise stated, no gladiator is permitted to take part in a match if he is more than two character levels higher than his lowest level opponent. A few also have additional rules for use in the Sands of Death game on p64.

ONE ON ONE

This is the simplest kind of gladiatorial fight and, indeed, for many pit fights is the only show on offer. Two combatants start in the arena, fighting until one is dead or yields. This type of match is generally only used to warm the crowd up for bigger events though it is also the only match of choice to pit two

INITIATIVE

Within the arena, Initiative is rolled for at the start of every new combat, rather than at the beginning of every match. For example, in a One on One match detailed below, each pair of opposing gladiators roll for initiative as normal, but it is re-rolled when a gladiator defeats his opponent and attacks another victorious combatant.

renowned gladiator champions against one another. One variation of this match is to have several One on One fights taking place in the arena simultaneously. When a victor emerges from one fight, he will wait until another fight has been completed and then engage the survivor. This continues until only one gladiator still stands having defeated the rest. This variation is very bloody but is also a good way for novice gladiators to make their mark and gain the attention of the crowd. A further variation is to have matched pairs enter the arena, working in concert to defeat every other pair.

Set up: Each gladiator will start within ten feet of his opponent. In multiple One on One combats, each individual fight will take place at least twenty feet away from any other. If matched pairs are being used, gladiators need not necessarily stay within a certain distance of one another, but they must completely defeat a pair before moving onto another, just as if they were single gladiators in an ordinary One on One.

Weapons & Armour: Random. Melee only.

Sands of Death: Each stable will put forward a single gladiator to enter the arena. These will then be paired off against their first opponent, with the two stables with the highest Fame score fighting each other. The two stables with the next highest Fame scores are paired off together, and so on. No gladiator is permitted to attack another if they are already engaged in combat. If there are an odd number of stables, the player with the lowest Fame score may either opt to not compete or face a suitable (same level) gladiator chosen from the table on p70. Such a non-player gladiator may be controlled by any player not currently fighting against the one being attacked. This may result in the non-player gladiator effectively switching hands throughout a match as he is passed on to one player, then another. If a paired match is rolled for, stables put forward two gladiators to fight side by side but otherwise follow the rules above.

ONE ON MANY

A popular match with the crowd, especially if a favoured gladiator champion is taking on several lesser combatants. The lone gladiator will either start in the centre of the arena, flanked or even surrounded by his opponents or, alternatively, will engage in combat as soon as he enters the arena.

Set up: The lone gladiator may choose whether to start in the centre of the arena or begin fighting as soon as he enters. The opposing gladiators start at least ten feet away from him or his place of entrance. The total levels of the opposing gladiators must be within one level of the character level of the lone gladiator.

Weapons & Armour: Random. Melee only.

Sands of Death: One randomly chosen stable master presents a single gladiator with which to face those of all the other stables.

CHAIN GANG

This is a vicious type of fight of which few gladiators truly master and is normally reserved for those stepping onto the sands of death for the very first time. Gladiators are paired and chained together, fighting against other chained pairs. The length of chain used is normally very short, being of no more than four or five feet, and thus greatly restricts a gladiator's manoeuvrability. Chain gangs have to be either adept at working together in perfect consort, a very rare occurrence, or one gladiator must be strong enough to completely dominate the other on his chain.

Set up: Each pair will start no closer than ten feet from any other.

Weapons & Armour: Random. Melee only.

Special Rules: No gladiator in a chain gang may be higher than second level. If using miniatures, gladiators on a chain must always be placed adjacent to one another. Gladiators on a chain lose all Dexterity bonuses, unless both are able to make a Wisdom check at DC 15 at the beginning of every round of combat. Dexterity penalties apply as

normal. Only weapons wielded in one hand may be used, as the hand chained is effectively useless for combat. A shield may be taken instead of a weapon.

If the two gladiators chained together opt to co-operate in the arena, they may otherwise fight as normal. However, opposing Strength checks must be made to determine which direction the chained pair move in if the gladiators are not co-operating fully for any reason (one may strongly disagree about attacking an ogre gladiator, for example). The winner will decide where they move, though it will be at half of their lowest base movement rate. In addition, if one of the gladiators is attacked, he may move his chained partner to receive the blow instead – again, an opposing Strength check is required for success. Uncooperative chained gladiators may never gain the bonus for charging.

Sands of Death: Each stable will put forward two chained gladiators to enter the arena as a pair – players may assume that such gladiators have been trained to co-operate when chained together.

MAGE KILLER

A rare show, as few mages will waste their time by setting foot inside an arena, but one guaranteed to amaze the crowd with huge explosions of magical energies as one or more gladiators attempt to defeat a solitary wizard or sorcerer. They must traverse the entire length of the arena to close with their enemy, all the while dodging the most powerful offensive spells the wizard has at his disposal. Few stable masters enjoy the prospect of sending their well trained gladiators against a competent mage but most are tightly bound by their contracts to the arena. Sometimes wizards with a grudge will agree to accept payment to resolve their disputes and thus an exciting mage duel may be on offer for the crowd though this is rarer still.

Set up: Combatants start at opposite ends of the arena, as far apart as is possible. The spellcaster is forbidden to use spells with large areas of effect (such as *fireball*), those that guarantee a hit (such as *magic missile*) or those that may potentially injure the crowd (such as *stinking cloud* if even a small breeze is present). Mercy may never be appealed for in mage killer matches.

Weapons & Armour: Gladiator's free choice. Melee only.

Set up: As for One on One or One on Many, depending on whether one gladiator is to face the creature or several. Creatures capable of flight are clipped or crippled, denying them this ability in order to protect the crowd and prevent their easy escape. Mercy may never be appealed for in a match involving monsters unless the beast handler is alive and present.

Weapons & Armour: Random.

Sands of Death: A monster is randomly chosen from those stables who own one, accompanied by a beast handler (see p37) from the same stable if one is available. The other stables must put forward gladiators to face the creature but their combined character levels may not exceed the creature's hit dice, plus the level of any beast handler. This may result in one or more stables being forced not to fight. The player owning the monster may move and control it as normal.

If no stable has a monster, select a suitable one from the list on p65, using the statistics in Core Rulebook III. When this creature is faced with multiple gladiators, it will start by attacking one at random. After this, it will always attack the gladiator who caused it the greatest amount of damage in the previous round.

Sands of Death: If a Mage Killer match is rolled for in Sands of Death, stable masters must each submit one gladiator of their choice to the arena. The combined levels of these gladiators will be equal to the character level of the wizard or sorcerer they face in the arena. Some pre-generated spellcasters are presented on p70 though players are also encouraged to use the character generation rules presented in Core Rulebook II to quickly create wizards and sorcerers of different levels.

BEASTS & MONSTERS

This match is often arranged in an identical manner to One on One or One on Many but the single gladiator is replaced by a vicious creature captured from the wild and trained to fight in the arena. The crowd delights in such matches for this is usually the only time they may ever see creatures such as a manticore or hydra. A rarer variation of this match will pit one monster against another but whilst such a fight may sate even the most bloodthirsty spectator, few can truly enjoy the spectacle without true gladiators taking part as well. Occasionally, a beast handler may accompany the monster into the arena.

BATTLES

Often put on as part of the mid-afternoon entertainment by arena managers in the build up to a grand finale, full-scale battles are popular with the crowd for their intensity and sheer amount of blood-letting. Often dressed in the armour and equipment of historical or mythical enemies, two teams of gladiators fight a full battle to the death. Each team will generally number between five and twenty gladiators though games commemorating special events may feature fifty or more on a team, given a large enough arena. Champion gladiators are rarely used for such butchery as it is seen as a waste of their talents though again, a new gladiator may easily make his name in such a confrontation.

Weapons & Armour: Random for each side – every gladiator on a team carries identical weaponry and armour. Melee only.

Special Rules: Only gladiators of 1st or 2nd level are allowed to compete in a battle. You may choose to fight out the battle using the standard D20 combat rules though this is likely to take a great deal of time with large teams of gladiators. Instead, you may use one of the D20-based mass combat systems currently on the market or alternatively, total the Strength and Dexterity scores of all gladiators on each team. Roll 1d20 for each gladiator and add this to the previous total. The team with the highest combined score will win the battle. Those on the winning side must make a Constitution check at DC 10 to survive the fight. Those on the losing side are presumed killed. Mercy may never be appealed for in battles.

Sands of Death: Stable masters detest using even their low ranking gladiators in battles as the rewards are relatively poor and there is a good chance that every one they send into the arena will be killed. To refuse, however, is to risk losing their arena contract altogether so there is little to do but send gladiators in. The arena manager provides all weapons and armour for battles but each stable master must donate one of his 1st and 2nd level gladiators. If more gladiators are required to even up the numbers on a team, use those presented on p70. Surviving gladiators of a battle receive 1d6 x 100 experience points, but no extra Fame.

SIEGES

A variation on the battle theme, arena managers arrange the construction of a wooden stockade or tower in the centre of the arena. A superior attacking force is given ladders and log rams and tasked to overcome the defenders inside.

Weapons & Armour: Attackers have a free choice of melee weapons and armour. Defenders have a free choice of missile weapons, a single medium or smaller melee weapon, and light armour.

Special Rules: Only gladiators of 1st or 2nd level are allowed to compete in a siege. The attacking force has twice as many gladiators as the defenders and will have as many ladders and log rams as they can carry. The defenders start inside a two or three storey wooden structure. If the quick combat resolution method detailed in battles is used, assume the defenders have twice as many gladiators as they actually do. Mercy may never be appealed for in sieges.

Sands of Death: As in the case of battles, stable masters detest using even their low ranking gladiators in sieges as the rewards are relatively poor

and there is a good chance that every one they send into the arena will be killed. To refuse, however, is to risk losing their arena contract altogether so there is little to do but send gladiators in. The arena manager provides all weapons and armour for sieges but each stable master must donate one of his 1st and 2nd level gladiators. If more gladiators are required to even up the numbers on a team, use those presented on p70. Surviving gladiators of a siege receive 1d6 x 100 experience points, but no extra Fame.

NAVAL BATTLES

Very few arenas are truly capable of staging naval battles as many have an underground tunnel complex that would be flooded if the arena was filled with water. Added to that, the logistical problems of moving the sheer amount of water required, even with magical aid, are immense. If willing clerics are present and available to the arena manager, it still takes vast numbers of them to fill even a small arena with enough water to float a sizeable vessel. Naval battles are thus extremely rare but they are always guaranteed to draw the crowds, particularly if the arena is situated in a city far from the sea. Such events are run in much the same way as battles, with each team of gladiators on board a small ship. Many variations abound, with no two naval battles ever being quite the same. More than two ships may be used, they may be armed with rams and siege weapons or they may be set alight before battle begins. An artificial island may be constructed in the centre of the arena complete with a wooden tower to combine naval battles with sieges. Vicious and powerful sea monsters may also be placed in the arena to further excite the interest of the crowd though this tends to be hideously expensive. In other cases, only a single ship may be used, with the gladiators fighting off a team of captured or magically controlled sahuagin or tritons.

Weapons & Armour: Random for each side – every gladiator on a team carries identical weaponry and armour.

Special Rules: Only gladiators of 1st or 2nd level are allowed to compete in a naval battle. It is suggested the rules for ship-to-ship combat and boarding actions in our forthcoming supplement *Seas of Blood* be used to act out naval battles in an arena. Mercy may never be appealed for in naval battles.

Sands of Death: Stable masters detest using even their low ranking gladiators in naval battles as the rewards are relatively poor and there is a good chance that every one they send into the arena will be killed. To refuse, however, is to risk losing their arena contract altogether so there is little to do but send gladiators in. The arena manager provides all weapons, armour and ships for naval battles but each stable master must donate one of his 1st and 2nd level gladiators. If more gladiators are required to even up the numbers on a team, use those presented on p70. Surviving gladiators of a naval battle receive 1d6 x 100 experience points, but no extra Fame.

SACRIFICIAL GAMES

Whilst the crowd values combats that pit gladiators of roughly equal strength against one another, so as to never be quite sure of the final outcome, arena managers are all too aware the primary attraction is blood-letting, the infliction of pain and suffering upon others. It is also understood that a cruel and sadistic streak in the crowd appreciates macabre humour. Thus were born the sacrificial games, matches where unskilled and unarmed captives are thrown into the arena to be met by vicious and hungry beasts, normally dire wolves or large wild cats. This provides a beneficial (to the arena) way of disposing of petty criminals or prisoners from an enemy nation. In some cities it also has religious connotations in that these helpless souls are sacrificed directly to a patron deity or, alternatively, are followers of some rival god with whom a war of faith is currently being fought.

There are no real rules with which to play out a sacrificial game – low level, unarmed captives will stand little real chance against these wild animals and thus you may assume none will survive. If player characters are ever thrown down into the arena, they will likely face perhaps a half dozen of these creatures whilst the crowd bays for their blood.

ARMED ON UNARMED

Such matches may sometimes arise as the result of handicaps in other fights between gladiators of uneven skill but occasionally they are scheduled as a fixed part of the games. One or more gladiators, generally very well armed and armoured will battle a more experienced one given only light armour at best and no weapon. A very small number of gladiators specialise in this form of unarmed combat and are always guaranteed to pull in the crowds.

Set up: As for One on One or One on Many, depending on whether one gladiator is to face the unarmed combatant or several. The total levels of the armed gladiators must be within one level of the character level of the unarmed gladiator. Gladiators will start within ten feet of one another.

Weapons & Armour: Armed gladiators have random melee weapons and armour. The unarmed gladiator has light armour and no weapons.

Sands of Death: A gladiator is chosen from one random stable. This is the unarmed gladiator. The other stables must put forward gladiators to face him but their combined character levels must be within one level of the unarmed gladiator's level. This may result in one or more stables opting not to fight.

BLIND FIGHT

Like Armed on Unarmed, this type of match may arise from a handicap but again, there are a few gladiators who specialise in this form of combat. An experienced gladiator is given heavy armour and a blindfold and then set against a gladiator of far lower ability with no armour. A common variation is to simply blindfold every gladiator, for the crowd delights in the sight of the combatants flailing wildly about with their weapons, hoping to make contact with an opponent before an unseen sword swing ends their own life.

Set up: Any match may be adjusted into a Blind Fight by giving each gladiator a blindfold, though battles would be fairly bizarre. The basic Blind Fight, however, pits one gladiator against a blindfolded one of up to twice his own character level. Gladiators will start within ten feet of one another and are assumed to have been led into the arena whilst blindfolded, so they must first find their opponent.

Weapons & Armour: Random melee weapons. Blind fighter has heavy armour, whilst opponent has none.

Special Rules: The rules for blind-fighting are detailed in Core Rulebook II.

Sands of Death: Blind Fights generated for Sands of Death will always involve every gladiator being blindfolded.

MOUNTED MATCHES

Speed of horse is always an exciting thing to witness, even within the confines of an arena. The very best of gladiators are capable of using steeds as an additional weapon, barging past the enemy, leaving them sprawling, before trampling over the broken body with iron-shod hooves. Mounted matches may take many different forms and any of the other matches listed here may be enhanced simply by giving each gladiator a mount – horses are the most readily available, though other creatures are often used too.

Set up: Any match may be adjusted into a Mounted Match simply by giving each gladiator a horse or similar creature. The basic Mounted Match, however, pits a team of those on foot against one mounted. The total levels of those on foot may be up to twice that of those mounted. Each team of gladiators will start on opposite sides of the arena, as far apart as possible. Mercy may never be appealed for in mounted matches.

Weapons & Armour: Random.

Sands of Death: Much to the chagrin of stable masters, each stable must provide its own mounts for its gladiators. Those stables unable to provide mounts may only take part in matches that pit mounted gladiators against those on foot.

CHARIOTS

There are few matches that can get the crowd jumping out of their seats as the chariot race can. Those gladiators who become skilled in controlling a very light vehicle drawn by incredibly fast horses are amongst the most respected in the entire arena and if a man can make his mark whilst in a chariot, his career is set. Chariot races are incredibly exciting to watch, for the sheer speed of the combatants is something rarely witnessed outside of the arena and the slightest mistake often results in a grisly and blood-soaked death. The successful chariot drivers are the true heroes of the arena, of that there can be no doubt. Chariots are also occasionally used against gladiators on foot, though there are few who would willing wager on even a renowned fighter being able to take on charging horses and spinning scythes.

Set up: Chariot races start with all competing chariots side by side – if there is no room, those with the highest Fame will be positioned ahead of those with lower scores. The track is normally an oval running around the outside of the arena with enough room for two chariots to travel side by side all the way around. However, other designs are also common, particularly the lethal 'figure-8'. Chariot games against gladiators pit a team of those on foot against one or more in chariots. The total levels of those on foot may be up to four times that of those in chariots. Each team of gladiators will start on opposite sides of the arena, as far apart as possible. Mercy may never be appealed for in a

match involving chariots. Full rules for chariots are given on p52.

Weapons & Armour: Random.

Sands of Death: Stables must provide their own chariots and horses – this can be an expensive business! Those stables unable to provide mounts may only take part in matches that pit chariots against gladiators on foot. Remember that every gladiator receives a point of Fame for just competing in a chariot race, win or lose.

JOUSTS

A popular pursuit of chivalric nobility, jousts also make for interesting diversions within the arena. If noble knights are putting on the show, they will do so with great pomp, resplendent in their finest armour and under family banners of immense honour. This is often the only way nobles can enter the arena as combatants in many cities without facing public disgrace. If gladiators are used for jousts, however, they will do so with no armour, carrying only a shield and a lance. Such jousts are fast and bloody, just as the crowd likes them, with terrific injuries being scored on each pass.

Set up: Gladiators will be paired off for this match and joust until one of the pair is killed or yields. The winner of this pair will then joust with a winner from another pair and so on until only one victor remains. These jousts are performed one at a time, not simultaneously, the better for the crowd to see the action. Mercy may never be appealed for in jousts.

Weapons & Armour: No armour except shield, and lances.

Special Rules: Full rules for jousting will be presented in our forthcoming supplement, *The Quintessential Fighter*. For now though, assume each gladiator receives a single simultaneous attack on each pass. Mounts may not attack in a joust, no matter what their type.

Sands of Death: Only stables with mounts are permitted to enter the joust. Each stable is permitted to enter more than one gladiator into a joust (and no, they may not share a horse) though be warned they may well end up fighting each other.

LORD OF THE PYRAMID

Occasionally used as a grand finale to a day's games, Lord of the Pyramid matches require the arena manager to arrange the construction of a large pyramid structure in the centre of the arena, with at least a dozen tiers or levels. Gladiators start on the lowest tier at equal distances from one another. The gladiator who reaches the top of the pyramid and defends it successfully against all the others wins. This normally requires the outright slaughter of all opponents though any gladiator may yield simply by climbing down off the pyramid. Arena managers sometimes create further problems for the gladiators by chaining some species of deadly monster to the highest level.

Set up: A pyramid of at least twelve levels is placed in the centre of the arena and gladiators start at roughly equal intervals along the edge of the lowest level.

Weapons & Armour: Random. Melee only.

Special Rules: The steps of the pyramid tend to be quite steep to further impede the gladiators. A Climb check at DC 10 must be made to go up each level. A gladiator may leave the match simply by climbing down off the pyramid or by being thrown off.

THE BLOOD BATH

The Blood Bath is an evocative title for a match that guarantees extreme violence and is often used as the final fight of a day's games. Few stable masters willingly participate in one unless they believe they hold a great advantage over their competitors as the very best of gladiators can easily become maimed or even killed in the Blood Bath. This match is basically a no-holds barred, anything goes event, with no restrictions on gladiator skill, weaponry, armour or even numbers. Stables often use such a deadly match to compete directly against one another over some point of business honour or even to force one another out of the arena altogether.

Set up: All gladiators start no closer than ten feet from each other. Any number of stables may compete, with each submitting any number of gladiators. There is a complete free choice of weapons, armour and other equipment and the rule of gladiators being within two levels of one another is disregarded for this match. Quite literally, anything goes! Mercy may never be appealed for in a blood bath.

Weapons & Armour: Gladiator's free choice.

DEVISING YOUR OWN MATCHES

These are just examples of the most common types of matches that many arenas will stage for the benefit of their crowds. Both players of the Sands of Death game and Games Masters are encouraged to devise their own more spectacular games – your imagination really is the only limit to what gladiators may be subjected to when they step into the arena.

Fights on weakened rope bridges above magically created rivers of lava certainly make for a stunning spectacle, as would chariots that have literally been set on fire. Whilst magic itself is usually banned for combatants, it can be readily adapted by ambitious arena managers to stage events and matches that will be truly memorable for the mob. Listed below are just a few other ideas to kick start your own creations;

† Two mages armed with Charm spells, attempting to force half a dozen gladiators to slay the other spellcaster.

† The archetypal mage duel, with two wizards or sorcerers battling it out with their most potent spells. This may also be an opportunity to settle once and for all who is the greater spellcaster – the sorcerer or the wizard. . .

† Chain gangs fighting over an arena riddled with hidden acid jets primed to erupt whenever they come too close.

† Catapult duels, with gladiators needing to assemble their weapon before aiming it at another team on the other side of the arena. Doing this with ballistae could be fun too.

† Bear fights, where experienc3ed gladiators face either a normal bear or a dire creature with no weapons and armour. The crowd will expect the blood to flow freely in such a match.

† Platforms raised above an acid bath, slowly sinking as gladiators fight on top. Only when one gladiator stands does the platform stop.

† A maze, constructed out of wood, or magically crafted out of stone, where gladiators run through, desperately trying to find their opponents before they are surprised themselves. The open-topped nature of the maze allows the crowd to view the action fully and even shout warnings to their favoured gladiators.

† Massacres where dozens of slaves are set against a handful of very experienced gladiators. Normally a scene for immense carnage (always a favourite with the mob), it has been known for the frightened slaves to unite and overcome the gladiators by sheer weight of numbers.

† An archery duel, where two gladiators face each other right across the length of the arena, attempting to fire as many accurate arrows as they can before their opponent finds his mark.

If you come up with any truly dastardly and devious ideas, send them in to us, together with any special rules. The very best will be immortalised on our web site for the whole world to see.

FAME, MERCY & THE CROWD

Should a gladiator survive his brushes with death in the arena, he will naturally attain much respect from the crowd and start the process of becoming a great celebrity within the arena. This is an inevitability and the best gladiators quickly learn to use this to their advantage. Gladiators are also dependant on the crowd when matches do not go as planned – very few gladiators are truly undefeated in the arena and whilst losing a fight often means death, some well-liked gladiators may find themselves in a position to appeal to both the crowd and the noble presiding over the games for mercy.

FAME

A well known gladiator who has attained his fame purely through his sword arm is eagerly awaited by the crowd. For hours they may patiently sit through numerous matches, waiting for the time when their favourite gladiator steps on to the sands of death. As he walks through the entrance to the arena, a deafening cry will erupt from the mob, increasing further in volume as he raises his weapon in salute. Many veteran gladiators live for this cry of recognition and, in time, they begin to seek it far more than mere gold. With the support of the crowd, the gladiator gains something far more important than riches – he gains reputation. With each parry of his shield and every thrust of his weapon, the crowd cheers him own, willing him to overcome his opponent. This can have a very real effect on the outcome of matches for a gladiator supported by the shouts and cries of thousands of spectators may well begin to feel invulnerable whilst his opponent may justly be intimidated by the constant boos and hisses that greet his appearance.

All gladiators have a Fame score, in addition to all their other abilities listed in Core Rulebook I. A gladiator with a high Fame score is renowned, able

Action	Fame Bonus
Every hit that scores 15 or more points of damage	+1
Defeating an opponent	+ enemy's level or Hit Dice
On victorious side in a match	+1
Competing in a chariot race	+1
Winning a chariot race	+1 per opponent beaten
Yielding to an opponent	-3/level of surrendering gladiator
Slaying an opponent appealing for mercy	-20

When gladiators meet in combat, compare their Fame scores. The gladiator with the highest Fame score is likely to enjoy quite a substantial advantage over his opponent, gaining a temporary morale bonus to his attack and damage rolls. This bonus will increase with greater amount of Fame, as shown below. However, it must be recalculated every time a gladiator begins to fight a new opponent.

Difference in Fame	Morale Bonus
1-4	0
5-8	+1
9-15	+2
16-25	+3
26-49	+4
50+	+5

This morale bonus may stack with other such bonuses, such as the Death Move feat, as noted elsewhere in this supplement.

Morale bonuses gained from the presence of a crowd only ever apply when a character is within the arena. They do not apply in regular adventuring.

to excite the crowd with his mere presence and is an absolute terror to face in the arena. One with a low Fame is just starting out on his career, or else is a mediocre gladiator at best, given to failing in matches and easily yielding to opponents. The latter rarely lasts long in any arena.

A new gladiator just walking into the arena for the first time starts with a Fame score equal to 10% of that of his stable's, rounded down. This is a one-time bonus and reflects the fact that a well known stable is always looked upon as producing worthy gladiators. Monsters who do not act as gladiators (those listed in italics on p65) never receive Fame.

From this point on, gladiators may only gain (or lose) fame through their actions within the arena, as shown on the table on the previous page. These bonuses are only ever added after a match has been fought, never during.

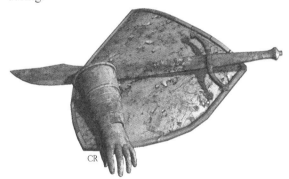

MERCY

Any gladiator may appeal for mercy to the crowd and possibly the noble presiding over the arena. To do so can represent a tremendous loss of face, as reflected in the Fame rules above, but if survival is granted, the gladiator will be alive and free to compete in the arena another day.

Any gladiator who is conscious and below 25% of his starting hit points may drop his weapon, fall to his knees before his opponent and raise his arm in appeal as a full round action. Whilst it has been known for bitter rivals to take advantage of such a position, such brutal action is frowned upon by the crowd, nobles, arena managers and stable masters alike and can seriously damage the reputation of a gladiator. Most back slightly away, looking to the crowd and the noble watching over the games to await their decision of whether his opponent is worthy of mercy. It is important to note here that a gladiator may not, of course, ask for mercy from an unintelligent monster.

When mercy is asked for, the crowd will erupt into howls of both support and derision, growing louder and louder until one side becomes dominant. Whilst the final decision is ostensibly the noble's he will usually look to the crowd to gauge popular opinion – thus, a gladiator's influence over the crowd can literally make the difference between life and death. A crowd will generally be lenient towards a gladiator who fought well but was completely outclassed by a more skilled opponent and will also tend to favour the most renowned combatants – nobody wants to see their hero instantly slain. Regardless of the verdict, a gladiator risks his whole career's reputation on begging for mercy but it is sometimes the only way to survive a dangerous match.

A gladiator begging for the crowd's lenience must succeed in a Mercy check at DC 10. This check is modified as follows;

Action	Modifier
Scored at least one hit on opponent	+1
Brought opponent to 50% or less of starting hit points	+5
If lower character level than opponent	+2 per level difference
If higher level than opponent	-3 per level difference
Fame	+10% of Fame score (round down)
Failed to score a single hit on opponent	-4

If the Mercy check is successful, the gladiator is removed from the arena immediately and is deemed to have lost the match. If it is failed, his opponent may attack immediately, automatically doing double damage in the first round of combat as he takes advantage of the gladiator's position. He also gains a +2 morale bonus to his attack and damage rolls against the yielding gladiator for the rest of the combat.

CHARIOTS

Whether in racing or direct combat, chariots are always guaranteed to entertain the mob. The sheer speed of such matches is breathtaking to behold and the power mustered by a chariot pulled by racing horses ensures plenty of the bloodshed the crowd desires to see in the arena. Charioteering is an even more dangerous pursuit for the gladiator as it introduces a wide range of lethal variables into any event – horses must be controlled, fast speeds allow precious little reaction time and an overturning chariot has ended the life of many combatants. But for any serious about advancing their career on the sands of death, chariot races provide a sure-fire method of gaining the attention of the crowd which is, ultimately, what every gladiator strives for.

Rules for setting up chariot races and matches are given on p47 but provided here are all the necessary tools you will need to conduct this unique form of combat within the arena.

CHARIOTS

All chariots require either light or heavy warhorses to pull such a weight at speed but there is a wide variation within the chariots themselves. Listed below are the three most common designs seen within arenas across the world. All vary from each other in several ways and are given the following characteristics;

Horses

This is how many light or heavy warhorses are required to pull the chariot. At the Games Master's option, other similar sized creatures may be used in their place.

Passengers

Chariots are basically simple three-sided carts with space for two or more passengers. This lists how many small or medium-sized creatures may ride in a chariot. Large creatures take the space of two medium-sized creatures. Creatures of huge size or greater may not ride in the chariots listed below.

Speed

This is the base speed of the chariot when pulled by the maximum number of horses. As horses are lost through combat or other means, the chariot's base speed moves to the next number on this line, thus gradually slowing down.

Hardness

As detailed in Core Rulebook I, this is the hardness of each chariot.

Hit Points

Every chariot has a number of hit points. When these are reduced to 0, the chariot is destroyed.

Turn Rate

The lighter a chariot is, the faster its driver can get it to turn at speed. The first number here is the turn a chariot can make, in degrees, when moving at normal speed. The second number lists how much it can turn when making a double move. No chariot can turn at running speed.

Cost

This is the base price a chariot costs to purchase. Some arenas may place a premium on chariots where they are relatively rare and any chariot may be upgraded as detailed on p55.

Weight

This is the base weight of a chariot, without passengers, cargo and horses.

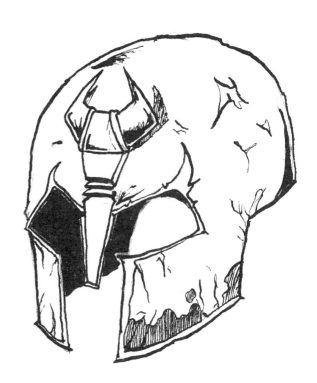

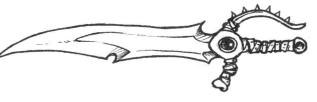

Cargo

All chariots may carry cargo instead of or in addition to any passengers. This amount is listed in this section. However, a chariot will always require a driver to control its movement.

Overrun

This is the base damage caused by the chariot when performing an overrun attack.

Light Chariot

Horses	2
Passengers	2
Speed	50 ft./40 ft.
Hardness	5
Hit Points	10
Turn Rate	90°/45°
Cost	300 gp
Weight	300 lb.
Cargo	800 lb.
Overrun	2d6

Heavy Chariot

Horses	2
Passengers	3
Speed	40 ft./30 ft.
Hardness	5
Hit Points	20
Turn Rate	45°/-
Cost	500 gp
Weight	450 lb.
Cargo	1,200 lb.
Overrun	3d6

War Chariot

Horses	4
Passengers	4
Speed	40 ft./40 ft./30 ft./20 ft.
Hardness	5
Hit Points	30
Turn Rate	45°/-
Cost	1,200 gp
Weight	600 lb.
Cargo	1,600 lb.
Overrun	4d6

Movement

Chariots move in initiative order in the same way as any mounted gladiator. There are, however, some important differences. A chariot may turn once at any point in its move, up to the amount listed as its turn rate. Any chariot may make this turn whilst making a normal or double move but none can normally turn whilst running.

In addition, chariots may 'drift' up to ten feet left or right for every full thirty feet they move forwards. This is performed as a free action and in no way impedes any other movements the chariot may perform.

A chariot driver may choose to whip his horses harder as a full round action. If he succeeds a Handle Animal check at DC 10, he may increase his base speed by ten feet for that round only.

Tight Turns

The driver may also attempt to get his chariot to turn in a much tighter fashion than may be advisable. A driver may choose to make two turns in a round instead of just one, though these must be made at the beginning and end of the move – they may not be made halfway through as a normal turn may. This is a full round action and requires the driver to make a Handle Animal check at DC 15 if he is moving at base speed and DC 20 at double speed. A single turn may be made at running speed, again with a successful Handle Animal check, this time at DC 30.

If these checks are failed, the chariot will automatically overturn at the start of the next turn, as covered below in Collisions and Overturning.

Combat

All passengers on board a chariot may make their normal attacks as if they were mounted. The chariot driver, however, must always dedicate at least one hand to controlling the horses and so may only fully utilise single-handed weaponry. Any passenger may make an attack at any point in their move, such is the speed of the chariot. This in no way affects the

number of actions they may perform each round. All chariots, no matter what their size, are assumed to take up a space five feet wide and ten feet long, with the horses directly ahead. Either passengers, horses or the chariot itself may be targeted by an attack if within reach or range, though passengers will receive the benefit of one-half cover for attacks to the front or sides of their chariot, as detailed in Core Rulebook I. They receive no benefit for attacks originating from the rear of their chariot.

If any horse is slain whilst pulling a chariot, it must be cut free within one round, as described under Collisions and Overturning, or the chariot will automatically overturn.

Sideswipes

The crowd loves the spectacle of two chariots racing neck and neck, the crews striking at each other as they attempt to manoeuvre their vehicles to damage the other or even remove it from the race altogether.

Any charioteer moving his vehicle alongside another chariot may choose to sideswipe it as a full round action. The drivers of both chariots must make an opposing Handle Animal check. The winner will cause damage upon the loser's chariot, as listed below;

Chariot Sideswipe

Damage	Critical Type	
2d4	20/x2	Bludgeoning

Chariot with Scythes Sideswipe

Damage	Critical Type	
2d8	19-20/x2	Slashing

AGAINST GLADIATORS ON FOOT

The passengers of a chariot may attack any gladiator on foot as if they were mounted. Those on foot may fight back as if the gladiators on the chariot were mounted. However, the driver of a chariot may either overrun his enemies, or make scythe attacks against them.

Overrun attacks are detailed in Core Rulebook I. If successful, such an attack will cause an additional amount of damage to the target equal to the Overrun score of the chariot, as covered above.
Scythe attacks are made as a chariot moves adjacent

to any suitable target and count as a melee attack action. The driver must make a Handle Animal check opposed by the target's Reflex check. If the target succeeds, he manages to dodge the attack. If the chariot driver wins, the scythes cut through the target, with devastating results. Use the scythe damage listed above, doubling the damage if the chariot is making a double move or faster.

COLLISIONS AND OVERTURNING

One of the most impressive sights a spectator may ever witness is that of a chariot moving at full speed then, for whatever reason, overturning. Wood, gladiators and horses all tumble and break apart as the entire mess is veiled by a cloud of dust and blood. Few ever survive such accidents and it is often only the skill of the charioteer that can avoid such tragedy.

Handle Animal checks are used by the driver to control his chariot whenever he attempts an extreme action or when a collision looms up ahead. The DC of such checks are listed below;

Action	DC
Cutting free a dead horse before chariot overturns	10
Swapping drivers whilst chariot is in motion	10
Hitting medium-sized creature or object	15
Hitting large sized creature or object	20
Hitting the arena wall	30

There is a +5 bonus to this check if the chariot is moving at base speed or slower and a –5 penalty if it is moving at running speed.

If the Handle Animal check is successful, the chariot neatly avoids the obstacle or swerves at the last moment. In the case of avoiding the arena wall, the chariot is placed alongside the wall, its driver having brought his horses up short at the last possible moment.

Games Masters are encouraged to use the above examples as a base should their players ever attempt an action not listed here. If the driver passes his check, he succeeds in the action he was attempting or manages to avoid tragedy, as appropriate. If he fails the check by 5 points or less, the chariot must move in a completely straight line for the next round. No turns or drifts may be attempted. If the chariot cannot move straight ahead for whatever reason (the arena wall being directly in front of the chariot, for example), then the chariot will automatically overturn. If he fails by more than 5 points, the chariot will overturn

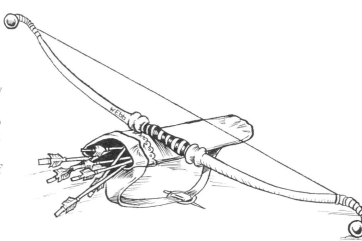

OVERTURNING

If a chariot overturns, the chariot itself, along with all passengers and horses, take an amount of damage equal to the Overrun score of the chariot. Passengers may make a Reflex check at DC 20 to halve this damage.

An overturned chariot, if it survives intact, takes 1d6 minutes to put right and re-hitch any living horses. This is far longer than most combats take within the arena and so is rarely done during a match. The combined Strength required is equal to the original hit points of the chariot.

CHARIOT UPGRADES

All chariots may be upgraded with fittings and devices designed to increase their lethality in some way whilst within the arena. The weight of these upgrades is deducted from the cargo capacity of the chariot in question. Many gladiators and stable masters spend a great deal of time refitting their chariots and one of the draws of the races, as far as the crowd is concerned, is to see exactly what

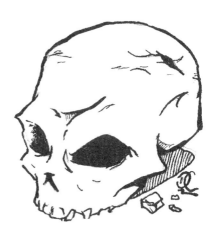

modifications have been made and then debate or gamble how they will effect the outcome of the match.

Metal Banding

Large metal plates or bands are strapped to the sides of the chariot, greatly increasing its resilience to damage. Whereas a normal chariot may be susceptible to strikes from axes and heavier weapons, it will take a determined and accurate hit to damage one reinforced with metal banding.

Metal Banding adds a bonus of +1 to a chariot's hardness score. *300 lb. 250 gp.*

Rear Shield

Most chariots are completely open backed, allowing for fast mounting and dismounting but providing no cover for attacks made to the rear. A rear wooden shield can be fitted to the rear of any chariot, effectively making it an enclosed box on all four sides.

A rear shield provides the crew with one-half cover to the rear, as well as to the sides and front but Reflex checks made by the crew if the chariot overturns are made at DC 30. *50 lb. 150 gp.*

Scythes

The most common upgrade of all and, indeed, few chariots will enter the arena without them. Fitted to the centre of the wheels of the chariot, these large blades are forged to be incredibly strong. Gladiators will intentionally drive past those on foot and other chariots in order to cause great damage by the spinning metal blades. This is the most offensive device that can be placed upon a chariot and the crowd always appreciates their

addition as they watch a huge spray of blood arc into the air as a chariot passes a target.

The rules for scythes are covered in the Combat section above. *100 lb. 100 gp.*

Weapons Rack

Many chariots have the cheap addition of a simple wooden weapons rack mounted inside, allowing crews ready access to a variety of weapons during a chariot race, much to the enjoyment of the crowd.

A weapons rack holds up to ten large or smaller weapons. *25 lb. 50 gp.*

Wheel Spikes

An incredibly difficult upgrade to perform on a chariot without ruining its fast speed, this consists of mounting a dozen or more metal studs or spikes to the wheel rims. These then cause even greater amounts of damage should the chariot ever overrun a target, but also have the benefit of digging into the sand of an arena floor, providing far better grip in tight manoeuvres.

Wheel spikes add 1d6 damage to a chariot's overrun score and grant a +2 competence bonus on any Handle Animal checks made by a chariot's driver. *50 lb. 500 gp.*

Sands of Death

Stable masters will no doubt have great fun competing in chariot races in the Sands of Death game on p64. Whilst the risks of placing their gladiators upon a chariot are great, the rewards almost make it worthwhile and they can certainly swing the odds further in their favour through the judicious use of chariot upgrades.

EXOTIC WEAPONRY

Gladiators are the stars of the arena and the lowliest slave has the chance to gain immense fame, even fortune. Just as important to the crowd as the individual gladiator is, however, are the weapons he takes into the arena. A whole industry can spring up around an arena, with weaponsmiths driven to conceive and construct more and more unlikely looking weaponry with which the gladiators may batter, pierce and slash each other with upon the sands of death.

Some gladiators gain recognition for using a particular type of unusual weapon, whilst others concentrate on becoming proficient with many types of weapons in order to keep their fans guessing. Whilst swords and axes may keep a crowd happy for a time, the successful arena manager soon learns that a varied choice of weaponry can excite interest as much as bringing in huge and expensive monsters. Whilst these weapons are born out of the necessity of entertainment, most are quite lethal and some enterprising adventurers take them out of the arena and into the wilds, especially if they are of a gladiatorial background themselves.

All the weapons listed here are considered exotic weaponry and will require proficiency for best use.

'Welcome to Hazzar's Emporium of Superlative Slayers. Venture inside and discover a true wealth of implements and devices all designed specifically for your victory upon the sands of death. . .'

Aclis

'A very unsophisticated weapon to be sure, but if the rope is well-concealed, it can give a hell of a surprise to an opponent who thinks he is out of range.'

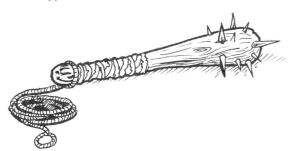

The aclis is simply a club attached to lightweight cord. Mainly used in melee combat, it may also be thrown, with the cord being used to drag the aclis back to be used again. Not an ideal weapon in normal combat, it may give an opponent a nasty surprise and if used by several individuals at once, can stall even a determined charge.

The aclis has a maximum range of 30 feet, as this is the length of the cord it is attached to. Dragging the club back after it has been thrown is a move-equivalent action.

Bolas, 3-ball

'Far heavier than the wimpy two ball set, this weapon requires a little more skill to use but can bring down a man with a single well placed throw.'

The 3-ball bolas is made from three heavy wooden or even metal spheres, connected by a length of chain or strong cord and is a weapon designed to both damage and trip an opponent at range.

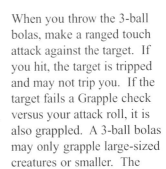

When you throw the 3-ball bolas, make a ranged touch attack against the target. If you hit, the target is tripped and may not trip you. If the target fails a Grapple check versus your attack roll, it is also grappled. A 3-ball bolas may only grapple large-sized creatures or smaller. The target can free itself from the bolas as a full round action.

Chakram

'A most impressive weapon, guaranteed to impress the crowd as well as do an incredible amount of damage against any opponent. In my opinion, the very first ranged weapon any gladiator should learn to use.'

The chakram is a heavy metal disk with razor sharp edges, designed not only to produce stable flight when spun towards an enemy, but also to return to the thrower if it should miss through the use of a strong cord wound around its centre. A heavy metal gauntlet (included in the purchase of a chakram) must be worn whilst wielding such a weapon, for it is more than capable of slicing off fingers and even hands as it returns at high speed to the thrower.

The maximum range of a chakram is 30 feet. It is used in the same way as any other ranged weapon but it will automatically return to the thrower whether it hits or misses. If the thrower is not wearing a metal gauntlet, it will cause normal damage on its return.

Light Harpoon

'More often seen carried by beer-swilling pirates and other nautical misfits, the light harpoon is a truly evil weapon. It is, then, perhaps obvious that it would be brought into the arena.'

This is a lightweight version of the weapon more commonly seen on high seas ships, used to defend the vessel against huge and terrible sea monsters, as well as capture larger fish for food. When used against a living target, the harpoon's barbed tip has a good chance of lodging inside an opponent, causing a great amount of pain and suffering. This, of course, makes them far easier to engage in regular combat.

If damage is inflicted with a light harpoon, the target must make a Reflex check at DC 10 + damage caused. If this is failed, the target is harpooned. Until the harpoon is removed, the target moves at half speed and may not charge or run. If the harpooned target attempts to cast a spell, a Concentration check must be made at DC 15 to avoid losing the spell. The Harpoon may be removed as a full round action but this will cause an amount of damage equal to that originally inflicted unless a Heal check is made at DC 15.

Mancatcher

'Vicious, underhanded and I love it! The mancatcher is more often seen in slaver trains but it has an ideal use in the arena when gladiators fight in pairs. One traps an opponent, holding him immobile, whilst the other moves in to finish him off.'

The mancatcher is a pole arm used to aid grapple attacks. By striking an opponent at range, he may be held immobile and unable to strike back. The

NEW EXOTIC WEAPONS

Weapon	Cost	Damage	Critical	Range Increment	Weight	Type
Small						
Chakram	35 gp	1d8	x3	10 ft.	3 lb.	Slashing
Spiked Helmet	25 gp	1d6	19-20/x2	-	3 lb.	Piercing
Wrist razor	25 gp	1d6	18-20/x2	-	5lb.	Slashing
Medium-size						
Aclis	1 gp	1d4	x2	10 ft.	3 lb.	Bludgeoning
Bolas, 3-ball	15 gp	1d6	x2	10 ft.	4 lb.	Bludgeoning
Light Harpoon	10 gp	1d8	x2	30 ft.	8 lb.	Piercing
Quad Crossbow	375 gp	1d10	19-20/x2	120 ft.	18 lb.	Piercing
Large						
Mancatcher	40 gp	special	-	-	12 lb.	Special

mancatcher also has sharp spikes within its large metal and spring-loaded grips that can cause a considerable amount of pain for anyone trapped within this weapon's grasp.

The mancatcher has a reach of ten feet. If used to grapple, it does not provoke an attack of opportunity and a +2 competence bonus is granted to the Grapple check. Once an opponent is grappled, you may opt to cause 1d3 points of damage automatically every round they are held.

Quad Crossbow

'An essential weapon when you absolutely, positively have to slay every last son of a bitch in the arena.'

A highly stylised ranged weapon that has the effect of always causing the spectator to look twice in order to make sure of what they are seeing. Built around a heavy and durable shaft, this weapon has four cross pieces, mounted in pairs and at right angles to one another. Four bolts may be loaded simultaneously and they are fired as with a normal crossbow, with the wielder simply turning the weapon ninety degrees after each shot to make ready the next bolt. This allows the rapid firing of what is the equivalent of a heavy crossbow, without the compromises of size and strength made with the far more common repeating crossbow.

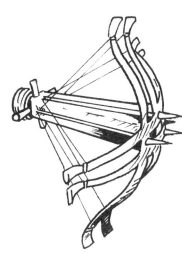

Up to four bolts may be fired according to a character's normal number of attacks without the need for reloading. No more than four bolts may ever be loaded at any one time in the quad crossbow. The quad crossbow uses standard crossbow ammunition as detailed in Core Rulebook I.

Spiked Helmet

'Ah, yes, the spiked helmet. An essential man-mangling device for the fashion conscious gladiator. Personally, I would prefer a good sword to this sort of foolishness, but you just cannot help some people.'

This is a strong and very well armoured helmet, with a long sharp spike mounted upon its top. Fashions and styles vary, but spikes have been seen measuring over a foot in length. It is an impractical weapon, but the crowd loves the use of such esoteric methods of killing and it can pack a surprising punch though is often best relegated to the status of a backup weapon.

Use of the spiked helmet counts as an unarmed melee attack. The spiked helmet deals double damage if used whilst charging.

Wrist Razor

'Cheap, relatively easy to use, and it doesn't even interfere with a swordsman's skill – the perfect backup weapon.'

A wicked looking weapon, it comprises of a sturdy metal band secured to the gladiator's wrist and forearm, with two or three large blades extending out above and beyond the hand. Such blades can be anything up to a foot or more in length and allow the wielder to fight in the style of a wild cat, scratching and clawing at his enemy, gouging great slashing wounds. They are usually worn as a pair and entire schools of fighting have sprung up regarding their use. More practical gladiators, however, often wear them in addition to using a more normal weapon, such as a sword. The wrist razors do not impede the use of any other weapon, though shields are impossible to carry, and provide a superior offence should the main weapon be lost through a disarming or similar disaster.

As the small column crested the brow of the frozen hill, they were at last able to look down upon their goal. The town was unimpressive, to say the least. Kai Pistorius just hoped that his man's information was good. There had been a war near this place. More like *in* this place, Pistorius thought, judging by the ramshackle state of the buildings. There was no wall to speak of, and the size would hardly merit more than a large village back home. He shrugged within the copious furs around his shoulders, nudging his horse forward. For the past 300 miles he had ridden in the comfortable calash which was now reduced to the rear of the convoy. Image was everything, after all.

The stiff northerly sea breeze whipped up the canvass sides of the prison wagon, exposing the bars, and looking like the sails might on the un-rigged longships in what passed for a harbour in these parts.

This had better be worth it, he thought.

They were greeted as they entered the town and, accompanied by several suitably imposing local soldiery, taken to a large wooden stockade which had been hidden from their approaching view. It smelt disgusting. In fact, it was a familiar smell to Pistorius, and one that made his heart well up with hope. It was the smell of beaten men, and beaten men made excellent gladiators. Also, they came cheap.

The negotiations had been harder than he had hoped, but no more than he had expected. The local warlord was a big fish around these parts, and Pistorius was obliged to act suitably impressed. Most of the prisoners were former warriors. Nothing special. Certainly not worth the trip. He bought five anyway. Two humans, a dwarf, a halfling and an orc. The orc was overpriced, but the crowd liked them.

Only as he was leaving did he catch sight of the small pit in the corner. Odd, he thought, turning to the northman. 'What's that for?'

'It's where we put the really bad ones,' his escort replied.

'Really bad?' The northman nodded in reply.

'Got one in there now?' another nod. Pistorius changed direction, and walked to the edge. As his shadow passed over the cavity it was greeted with a savage scream.

'Half mad, that one,' said the escort. 'Killed two of my men with his bare hands. He'll die in there.'

'Oh, I think not,' contradicted the stable manager, his mind already thinking ahead. This journey was suddenly looking a whole lot better. 'What's his name?'

The northman paused, frowning. 'They call him Tharg.'

DIRTY TRICKS OF THE SANDS

The arena is the scene of bloodshed, hope and utter desperation. Even the most renowned gladiator may meet his match from new opponents he faces for the very first time and there is always pressure from below as the less experienced seek to make their own names in front of the crowd with his death. The consequences of failure in the arena are total and final, with few matches allowing the loser to walk away with his life. Even begging for mercy, a truly debased act for a famous gladiator, is no guarantee of being spared.

It is thus perhaps inevitable that, throughout all the centuries arenas have existed, gladiators have gradually devised many methods of either fooling the crowd or bringing a quick, if not particularly noble end to their enemies. The dirty tricks, as they are called, of the sands are rife throughout many of the larger arenas and even though a city's nobles may seek to bring about their end with promises of execution, still they persist. For many gladiators, they represent the only hope of survival once they set foot within the arena.

Any of the dirty tricks listed below may be attempted by players and their opponents, provided they have the money and the courage to pull them off. Games Masters are also welcome to come up with more, greatly elaborated schemes with which to test their players and we have no doubt that the players themselves will prove the most devious of all when it comes to such planning.

There is always a price to pay if a gladiator is discovered attempting foul play and we have listed below suitable penalties to hard-earned Fame should this ever be the case. This is representative of what will happen to the gladiator's public opinion in the vast majority of arenas and is the penalty used in the Sands of Death game on p64 should stable masters ever feel the need to even the odds in their favour. However, in regular role-playing sessions, the Games Master is welcome to be far more severe. In arenas dominated by a totalitarian society that views the games as a method to control its population, this trickery may well result in immediate arrest and execution as an example to others.

Bleeding Damage

The causing of grievous wounds that continue to bleed long after dealt is not strictly a dirty trick and, indeed, the crowd often enjoys the mass of blood that results. However, it is something many other gladiators take a very poor view of – if a man must die in the arena, let it be quick. There is no need to prolong pain and suffering.

Bleeding damage may only be caused by slashing weapons. A gladiator must announce his attention to cause such before he strikes and suffers a –2 penalty to his attack roll as he angles his weapon with precision to cause the greatest amount of damage. If he manages to hit his target, he makes a Slashing check at DC 20, with the damage actually caused as a bonus modifier. If successful, the target will lose 1 hit point per round from the wound as it continues to bleed. This only stops after 10 – the target's Constitution modifier rounds, a *cure* spell is applied or a Heal check is made at DC 15. Multiple wounds may cause cumulative bleeding damage. Plants, constructs, undead or outsiders are immune to this attack.

Blood Bags

Gladiators will try many things to avoid death and the use of blood bags is especially common where slaves are not used for the arena, but organised guilds are set up to run the games. A leather sack or bladder is filled with the blood from an animal and then concealed on some part of the gladiator's body, hidden from the crowd and other observers. Another gladiator will then strike the bag during the match, thus releasing the blood as his opponent makes a great show of sinking to the ground and dying. This does, of course, rely on the total co-operation of an opposing gladiator, but many are known to make pacts with one another, promising to repay the favour one day.

A gladiator may purchase and hide a blood bag somewhere on his body for just 4 gp. However, it will also require the total co-operation and knowledge of his gladiatorial opponent in the match it is to be used and this may be particularly difficult to achieve, especially if he is from a rival stable.

The blood bag may be burst on any successful hit the opponent wishes and the 'dying' gladiator must then make a Perform check at DC 15 to fool the crowd with his death. In addition, his stable master will also have to make bribes to the slaves who

carry bodies off the sands and their owners to conceal the secret. This will take an additional 1d6 x 100 gp.

If the gladiator fails to convince the crowd of his death, he is likely in very serious trouble, as the use of blood bags is seen as the height of cowardice by the mob and it certainly deprives them of true bloodshed. In more civilised societies, this will result in the loss of 20 Fame points. In other, more wild places, it is highly unlikely the gladiator or his accomplice will make it out of the arena alive.

Blowpipe

In an attempt to even the odds against a particularly well-respected opponent, less honourable gladiators sometimes carry a small but well-crafted blowpipe into the arena, little longer than the palm of their hand. Easily concealed, such a weapon is loaded with a single poison dart that the gladiator will attempt to fire at his opponent whilst in the midst of another action, so as to hide his intent. The true

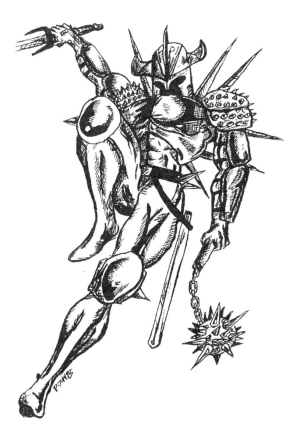

masters of this trick are often able to fire the dart without even their opponent recognising what they have done, let alone the crowd far away in the stands.

The shortened blowpipe will cost a mere 3 gp, but the poisons used upon the darts are likely to be far more expensive - Games Master may create their own or those listed as injury poisons in Core Rulebook II may be readily used. Only a single dart may be carried into the arena, as the blowpipe must be loaded and ready to fire as the gladiator steps on to the sands – he will not be able to reload without giving away what he is doing.

Normally poisons are incredibly hard to locate and purchase, but players may assume that stable masters in the Sands of Death game on p64 have a ready source of underworld contacts able to procure such items.

A ranged attack roll is made as normal when firing this blowpipe, though the maximum range is ten feet. If successful, the effects of the poison used are applied as normal. However, the firing gladiator must also make a Bluff check at DC 15 to avoid the suspicion of the crowd. Failure will result in the loss of 10 Fame points.

Caltrops

In many arenas, these small metal spikes are not strictly considered illegal and the crowd may even applaud their use, so long as the gladiator concerned is somewhat overmatched by his opponent in the first place. The sight of a large gladiator hobbling after his cunning halfling opponent has brought tears to the eyes of many crowds before now.

The purchase and use of caltrops is covered in detail in Core Rulebook I.

Pulling Damage

Whether out of concern for a friend or merely amusement and sport, gladiators have been known to pull their blows. Intentionally not putting as much effort into each swing or thrust, they reduce the injuries their weapons cause. This often happens when two friends have been forced to fight, but skilful gladiators, the true showmen of the arena, also tend to do it when faced with an overmatched opponent in an effort to prolong the match and thus give the crowd a better spectacle. After an attack roll has been made, a gladiator may opt to pull the damage. He must then specify a modifier to his damage roll. However, crowds rarely like to see a gladiator so obviously putting less than his full weight behind each stroke of the sword and so a Perform check at DC 10 must be made to hide the fact that a greater amount of damage is not being done. The actual damage caused is used as a bonus modifier to this check. A gladiator discovered pulling his damage will immediately face cat calls and derision from the crowd, as well as lose 5 points of Fame.

Sands & Powder

Though very different in effect, the application of sand and dangerous powders within the arena is much the same. All crowds enjoy the sight of a gladiator scooping up sand and then hurling it in the face of his enemy before launching a devastating attack but cunning gladiators have seized upon this tactic to employ distracting or even lethal powders against an opponent.

Hurling either sand or powder at an opponent is a move-equivalent action that generates an attack of opportunity. It may only be done to an enemy within five feet and, obviously, a free hand is needed to perform this action. To hurl either sand or powder, a ranged touch attack must be made.

Sand

Sand is freely available in most arenas – after all, a gladiator need only bend and scoop up a handful. A successful attack will partially blind the target, who will then suffer a –1 penalty to his next attack roll. Anyone attacking him during this time will receive a +1 bonus to their attack rolls.

Irritation Powders

Powders causing sustained periods of irritation are also available, normally for around 250 gp per dose. If the ranged touch attack is successful, the target must make a Fortitude check at DC 10 or suffer the effects of sand above for 1d6 rounds. When powder has been used in this fashion, it is usually fairly obvious to the crowd that foul play is at work. Any gladiator successfully employing irritation powders will lose 1d6 points of Fame.

Deathwatch Powder

Against truly dangerous opponents, a gladiator may go to the unusual length of employing powders that cause severe pain, weakness, even death upon inhalation. The Deathwatch powder is one such substance often seen within the larger arenas and typically costs around 1,800 gp. It counts as a poison – Inhaled DC 18, 1d6 Con, 2d6 Con. Alternatively, the inhaled poisons in Core Rulebook II may be used instead.

Using these powders is not without its own dangers for the wielder, as the merest breeze can blow some back into his own face as he hurls it at an enemy. If a 1 is rolled for the ranged touch attack, the thrower must make a Reflex check at DC 15 or be immediately effected by his own powder.

The Fates entered the arena with a jingle of sparkling harness and glittering steel. They circled the arena in their chariot allowing their adoring public a good look before the match began. They were the only undefeated women to ever stride the sands of death. There were still a few that believed 'The Fates' luck would run out. The Fates did not believe in luck. They practised more than any other gladiators did, therein lay their good fortune.

Hamli allowed herself a small smile as the roar of the crowd overpowered the trumpets and drums. She held the reigns of the gleaming chariot loosely in her left hand, her right hand resting loosely on the hilt of her sword. Her black armour seemed to absorb light. Rose and Gilda stood behind her to either side in shining white. The team of horses were similarly decked, beautifully matched pairs of black and white steeds that the women had worked with tirelessly.

At a pre-determined spot the elves vaulted over the front of the chariot onto the backs of their horses, slipped the knots of the harness and circled to flank the chariot, their petite paleness contrasting sharply with the powerful black flanks of the matched warhorses. The cheers of the crowd surged to a deafening howl.

In her peripheral vision, Hamli saw one of their opponents begin to pray.

Part III
SANDS OF DEATH

There are many reasons a man may praise the existence of a grand arena. To the commoner, it is relief from a life of drudgery, a chance to see bloodthirsty combat portrayed as the ultimate in entertainment. A city ruler looks to the arena to suppress the more violent tendencies of his population and curb their attention away from problems of state that may otherwise make them ungovernable. For the slave, the sands of death offer both the promise of violent release from the chains of servitude but also the elusive lure of freedom.

Others look for profit. These are the stable masters, traders in the flesh of others for monetary gain. They instinctively know a good gladiator on sight and scour the stocks of slavers and prisons to find the most valuable commodity of any arena – men and women who can fight, and fight well. Through shrewd business decisions that would shame a wealthy merchant and the careful grooming of gladiators within their stable, they may gain immense fortunes. Whilst a gladiator has the slim chance of becoming rich himself if he survives enough fights, his stable master is likely to make ever increasing amounts of gold no matter what the final outcome on the sands of death.

SANDS OF DEATH

This is a game based on the D20 combat system for two or more players. Each player takes the part of a stable master, buying and cultivating gladiators to take part in a range of fights for the entertainment of a blood-craving crowd. Competing against the other stable masters, a player must ensure he has the best gladiators, the finest quality equipment and the greatest luck in the arena if he is to succeed above the others. Each player has a Stable Master Record Sheet, as shown on the rear inside cover. This sheet is not considered 'secret' during the game and may be inspected by other players at any time.

SETTING UP

Each stable master starts with 5,000 gold pieces with which he must buy gladiators and equip them with weapons and armour. Several sets of each will likely be required for every gladiator as many of the

fights they will engage in have strict rules as to what is and is not permitted. There is no limit to the amount of gladiators you may purchase other than the gold pieces you have. The prices for them are listed below;

Race	Gold Pieces
Human	500
Elf	600
Dwarf	750
Half-Elf	550
Half-Orc	800
Gnome	450
Halfling	450
Goblin	350
Hobgoblin	600
Kobold	300
Orc	600

Humans, elves, dwarves, half-elves, half-orcs, gnomes and halflings are all generated normally as if they were player characters, gaining skills and feats as detailed in Core Rulebook I, though they do not receive any starting money or equipment. They automatically start at 1st level as slaves, as detailed on p35. Alternatively, if you are in a rush to start playing, you may use the sample gladiators on p70 as a starting point. Goblins, hobgoblins, kobolds and orcs all start with the statistics provided for their race in Core Rulebook III - they do not, however, receive any weapons and equipment as these must be paid for as normal by the stable, but will have the maximum possible hit points (orcs start with 8 hit points, for example).

Any stable master may purchase previously trained gladiators, however. Warriors and barbarians from primitive tribes are often captured for the arena, whilst some fighters willingly sell themselves into slavery in order to gain fame and fortune as a gladiator. Unlucky rogues may find themselves removed from imprisonment only to be sold to a stable master looking for an agile combatant. The additional costs for these character classes, on top of that for the race listed above, are detailed below;

Class	Gold Pieces
Arena Slave	+100
Warrior	+250
Rogue	+500
Fighter	+1,000
Barbarian	+900

An arena slave may take advantage of the Born to Fight rule on p35.

Weapons and armour are bought from the equipment lists on 57, Core Rulebook I and any other supplements the players agree to use. Masterworked items may be purchased but magic items may not. Players may find it beneficial to consider the purchase of horses and chariots even at this early stage of the game.

Names should be chosen for each gladiator and listed in the appropriate section of the Stable Masters Record Sheet. We have noticed that gladiators with names always seem to last longer within the arena than those without – you have been warned!

Monstrous Gladiators

A stable master may sometimes be drawn to providing monsters for the arena as the contract rates can be very lucrative. Such creatures, however, are expensive and difficult to both purchase and maintain, and few can effectively fight a truly experienced gladiator. They do ultimately provide a great show for the crowd though.

The monsters permitted for use by stable masters are listed below though more may be added if all players are in agreement. No monster may start with a character class and simply uses the statistics given in Core Rulebook III – they do not, however, receive any listed weapons and equipment as these must be paid for as normal by the stable. Those in italics may never earn experience points or Fame and may only be used in matches that specifically call for a monster. Those not in italics are bought as monsters but in all other respects are treated in the same way as any other gladiator in that they are free to compete in any match (use their effective level to pit them against other gladiators, i.e. their starting hit dice plus any character levels they attain) and may gain experience and Fame. Unfortunately for the stable master, though, they still count as monsters for the purposes of the expenses on p69.

Ankheg, bugbear, *bulette*, *carrion crawler*, centaur, *chimera*, *chuul*, *dinosaur*, *dire animal*, ettin, *gargoyle*, giant, gnoll, *hydra*, lizardfolk, *manticore*, minotaur, ogre, *owlbear*, troglodyte, troll, *worg*.

The price for these monsters is based on their Challenge Rating as depicted in the table below. Normal animals may also be purchased for one half this price.

Challenge Rating	Gold Pieces
1	1,250
2	2,500
3	4,000
4	6,000
5	8,000
6	10,000
7	13,000
8	16,000
9	20,000
10+	+5,000 per CR

Beginning Fame

A stable's Fame score is very important for its master for this, above all else, determines how well his gladiators are doing on the sands of death. A stable with a high Fame score will immediately sway the crowd as a prized gladiator steps into the arena and will be able to influence the arena manager to put forward more desirable matches.

A stable starts with a Fame score of 1d6. If any monstrous gladiators are included in the stable at this point, a +2 bonus is awarded. If any goblins, hobgoblins, orcs or kobolds are included in the stable, there is a +1 bonus to the Fame score. These bonuses are one-off awards and are not given for *each* such gladiator in the stable. Read more about Fame on p50.

A stable's own Fame score is the total of all the Fame of its gladiators, plus its initial Fame score. When a gladiator gains his freedom, is killed or otherwise leaves the stable, he takes most of his Fame score with him. However, the stable retains 10% of his Fame score as the memory of where this gladiator was trained and raised will live on. Over time, stables can gain a very great reputation for producing gladiators who consistently excel in the arena.

TURN SEQUENCE

Each turn in Sands of Death represents a single day at the games. Stable masters are contracted by the arena manager to provide a certain amount of gladiators for a specified number of matches. Refusal is not an option and even when stable masters are presented with a match likely to end the careers of one or more of their gladiators, they have little choice but to comply. Failure to do so will result in the stable master having his contract to provide gladiators revoked – he will be out of the business and out of the game!

Stable masters will be called upon to engage in four matches each turn, all of which are randomly generated. At the end of these four matches, stable masters may challenge one or more of their opponents to a match of their own choosing. Each turn follows the sequence detailed below.

Step One

The stable master with the highest Fame score rolls on the Random Match Table on the opposite page to determine which match will be played next. If any stables have an identical amount of Fame, roll a die to decide who gains priority in this match. All stables able to compete must do so – they may only refuse if they do not possess the required equipment (horses or chariots, for example) or if they cannot provide a gladiator of a suitable character level. This will no doubt involve a lot of pleading and grovelling to the arena manager but, thankfully, this is not handled within these rules.

Step Two

The stable master with the highest Fame score then chooses which gladiator(s) he will put forward in the match, following the rules in Types of Matches on p42. He may also choose what part his gladiator(s) will take in a match – being the lone gladiator in a One on Many, for example. The other stable masters do the same, in descending order of Fame. If there is still room for more gladiators (in a Mage Killer match, for example, where the total levels of gladiators do not match the mage assigned to fight) after all stable masters have decided who is going to enter the match, start the process of submitting gladiators again, starting with the stable with the highest Fame score. Pre-match advertising also takes place at this point.

Step Three

Stable masters are encouraged to introduce their gladiators before a match begins, detailing the weapons and armour they are carrying. There are two ways to do this;

'My half-orc warrior Tharg carries a battle axe and wears leather armour.'

Or. . .

'Tharg the Mighty strides into the arena, whirling his huge axe above his head as he challenges all comers to die at his hand. His battered leather armour is a testament to the many matches he has fought and won.'

We'll let you decide which is the more fun.

The match is then fought, again using the rules for Types of Matches on p42.

Step Four

The results of the match are calculated, slain gladiators crossed off the Stable Master's Sheet and experience points and gold pieces awarded, as detailed below. Note that stable masters may not purchase new equipment and gladiators, nor may gladiators gain new character levels until step seven.

Step Five

Steps 1-4 are repeated three more times so a total of four matches are played in this fashion.

Step Six

Once these four matches are complete, the stable with the highest Fame score may choose to challenge one or all of the other stables to a match of his choosing. Such matches need not be those listed on the Random Match Table and, indeed, he is free to conceive of his own match with his own rules. The other stable masters are, however, under no obligation to accept the challenge. If the stable master with the highest Fame score does not make such a challenge, then the stable master with the next highest Fame may make a challenge in the same fashion. This continues until a match is fought or it is determined that no stable master wishes to issue a challenge.

Random Match Table

D20	Match		Variation
1-7	One on One	1-14	Standard One on One
15-16	Matched Pairs		
17-18	Blind Fight		
19-20	Mounted		
8-10	Chain Gang		
11-12	One on Many	1-16	Standard One on Many
		17	Chain Gang (the Many are chained in pairs)
		18	Unarmed on Armed
		19	Blind Fight
		20	Mounted
13-14	Beast & Monsters	1-18	Standard Beasts & Monsters
		19	Chain Gang (gladiators are chained)
		20	Mounted
15-16	Chariot	1-16	Chariot Race
		17-20	Chariot against Foot
17	Joust		
18	Lord of the Pyramid		
19	Mage Killer		
20	Battle	1-10	Standard Battle
		11-15	Siege
		16-20	Naval Battle

Permitted Armour

Once a match has been decided, roll on the table below to determine the maximum armour type permitted. This roll will apply to every gladiator competing unless the rules of the match specify otherwise. Stables unable or unwilling to provide their gladiators with the armour type rolled for must still compete with lighter or no armour.

D20	Armour
1-7	None
8-14	Light
15-18	Medium
19-20	Heavy

Permitted Weaponry

Next, the permitted weaponry for gladiators must be rolled for. Unless match rules specify weapon types, *each* gladiator must roll on this table separately, adding their Fame to the die roll, thus creating a great variety of arms that will be taken into the arena. Stables unable or unwilling to provide their gladiators with the weapon rolled for must still compete with a smaller weapon. Shields may be used freely where possible and more than one weapon may be taken by a gladiator, so long as both are permitted by the table below.

D20	Weapon
1-3	None
4-6	Tiny
7-14	Small or medium
15-18	Large
19-20	Free choice

Step Seven

Once the four contracted matches and any challenges have been resolved, surviving gladiators are automatically healed back up to their starting hit point level and may gain new character levels if they have attained sufficient experience. Stable masters must pay their expenses and may purchase new equipment and gladiators. A new turn then begins with step one.

FIGHTING MATCHES

All matches are resolved using the D20 combat system in Core Rulebook I. Any additional rules detailed in this book (such as the Gladiatorial Feats on p40, for example) are also permitted, as are any of those in other supplements that all stable masters agree to use.

Miniatures may also be used, or not, as the stable masters collectively agree. Many of the larger matches greatly benefit from the use of miniatures, however.

Hit points are not regained between matches unless a healer is present. All hit points are, however, regained after each turn (day of games). A gladiator reduced to negative hit points is considered slain – there is no chance for a healer to reach him in time as he bleeds to death in the centre of the arena.

WINNING MATCHES

At the end of every match, there will be a number of slain or, at very best, badly wounded gladiators, along with the proud victors. Each stable gains a contract rate for every gladiator they put into the arena, though victory in matches naturally leads to the greatest rewards. With victory comes both fame and fortune, the latter being used to purchase better equipment and even new gladiators to replace those lost.

Rewards of Gold

After each match, every stable that took part will earn the following amounts of gold pieces;

Each gladiator who took part – 500 gp/level
Each gladiator who used exotic weaponry – 100 gp
Each defeated enemy – 500 gp/level

Gladiators themselves get a 20% portion of the

amounts listed above. This goes into their own purse which is recorded on the Stable Master's Sheet. This purse is usually used by the gladiator to buy his own freedom (see below). If the gladiator is slain though, the purse is also lost, perhaps to be used to support his family or, more likely, simply confiscated by the arena manager. It is important to note that this money is *not* the property of the stable master!

The remaining gold goes directly to the stable master to do with as he sees fit. The monsters listed in italics on p65 do not receive the 20% take of the winnings – the stable receives it all.

Experience Points

Gladiators themselves also earn experience points for the opponents they defeat in the arena. Using the Experience Point Awards table in Core Rulebook II, each gladiator will receive an amount of experience points for every enemy they defeat, using the enemy's character level or Hit Dice as the Challenge Rating. If several gladiators are fighting on the same side (in a Beasts & Monsters match, for

example), all survivors will share the experience point awards equally.

Gladiators are free to multiclass when they go up levels, but are restricted to warrior, fighter, rogue, barbarian or any prestige class.

A gladiator on the winning side in a match gains a 50% bonus on all the experience points he earns by defeating his enemies.

Mercy

It happens to every stable master sooner or later. A prized gladiator will walk into the arena and through either bad luck or lack of skill, will be brought close to defeat. In such circumstances, a stable master will bellow at his gladiator to kneel and appeal for mercy to the crowd.

The rules for appealing for mercy are detailed on p51, but if a gladiator appeals for mercy, his opponent *must* wait to see the reaction of the crowd – he may not simply wade in and finish him off.

HEALING GLADIATORS

Ordinarily, gladiators do not heal hit points between matches and have to wait until the next turn where they can rest and regain their health. However, a stable with a competent healer has a tremendous advantage over its competitors. A good healer can patch a gladiator up in a very short amount of time, even going as far as to provide mind-altering herbs that can allow a combatant to forget just how badly hurt he really is.

The services of a healer may be retained by a stable for 600 gp and start with a Heal skill rank of 4. This skill rank will go up by one point every other turn. A stable may retain as many healers as it can afford. It is important to note that these healers are not slaves for the stable master to bully as he sees fit, but private individuals of great skill. The stable master is merely paying them to not seek employment with a competitor.

A healer (or gladiator with the Heal skill) may heal an amount of hit points each to their skill rank after each match. This amount may be applied to a single gladiator or spread amongst several, as required.

Alternatively, a stable master may be willing to make generous donations to local temples and churches in order to make use of clerics and priests and their divine magic. Any healing spell may be purchased by the stable master at a cost of the

Spell's level, multiplied by the level of the cleric (this is the stable master's own choice, but he must be capable of casting the spell desired) and this total then multiplied by 100 gold pieces. Any experience point costs are also added to this total.

A stable master may even be in a position to purchase a spell such as Raise Dead though be warned, this can be very, very expensive.

EXPENSES

Every stable master in the arena can be heard to constantly grumble over how much his gladiators are costing him each and every day. The fact that their income comes primarily from the same gladiators seems lost to many of them. After each game turn, every stable master must pay the amounts of gold listed below to sustain his gladiators and beasts, maintain their weaponry and armour, and retain the services of his all important healers.

Expense	Gold Pieces
Gladiator	10 gp/level + 10 gp per point of Gladiator's Fame
Monster	100 gp/Hit Dice
Healer	25 gp/rank in Heal
Horses	20 gp

Gladiators with negative Fame (yes, it can happen!) simply play 10 gp/level – you do not receive money for having a poor gladiator!

If these expenses cannot, or will not, be paid, the stable will start to feel the effect of its master's penny pinching. Gladiators and monsters will suffer a cumulative –1 morale penalty to both attack and damage rolls every time their expenses are not paid. Healers will leave the employ of the stable immediately and horses will suffer 5 hit points of damage. Whilst healers will not return to a stable that has refused to pay them, the penalties applied to gladiators, monsters and horses will be immediately removed once the stable master begins paying their expenses once more.

FREEDOM

There are two ways a gladiator may gain his freedom from slavery by successfully competing in the arena. Any gladiator who attains a character level of 10 is automatically set free by the arena manager or, more likely, the ruler of the city. Such a

gladiator will be well renowned and the 'grand gesture' of giving him his freedom will raise the people's opinion of the ruler. The stable master has no choice in this. The gladiator is crossed off the Stable Master Record Sheet, taking his purse of gold with him.

However, the gladiator may be able to buy his freedom from the stable master. This may happen at any time the stable master chooses – the gladiator is crossed off the Stable Master's Sheet and the stable master in turn receives all the gold in the gladiator's purse.

TRADING

Stable masters are often greatly jealous of the gladiators they groom and train, rejoicing in every victory and jeering at their competitors after each successful match. Unknown to those not within the inner circles of an arena though, is the fact that a lot of trading does go on between rival stable masters. At the end of the day, they have more in common with each other than any may care to admit, for they

Starting Gladiators

All the gladiators listed here may be used instead of using the character generation rules of Core Rulebook I if players desire a quick and speedy game. You are likely to find that whilst these gladiators do not particularly excel in any one area, they are also balanced enough not to suffer heavily in any one regard. They are all 1st level slaves, though players may opt to upgrade them to warriors, rogues, fighters or barbarians using the costs listed on p65. Skills are likely to need adjusting and feats may be swapped out and replaced with others as players desire but this will still be quicker than generating a gladiator from scratch.

Heiron Blitzer
Human Slave
Str: 15, Dex: 13, Con: 14, Int: 8, Wis: 10, Cha: 12; HP: 8; Base AC: 11; BAB: +2; Fort: +2, Ref: +1, Will: +0; Skills: Handle Animal +5, Swim +6; Feats: Cleave, Power Attack

Rajnar Ironfist
Dwarf Slave
Str: 15, Dex: 13, Con: 16, Int: 8, Wis: 10, Cha: 10; HP: 9; Base AC: 11; BAB: +2; Fort: +3, Ref: +1, Will: +0; Skills: Climb +6; Feats: Taunt

Dasaeyar Crow
Elf Slave
Str: 15, Dex: 15, Con: 12, Int: 8, Wis: 10, Cha: 12; HP: 7; Base AC: 12; BAB: +2; Fort: +1, Ref: +2, Will: +0; Skills: Handle Animal +2, Listen +2, Search +1, Spot +2, Use Rope +5; Feats: Dodge

Zook Duergal
Gnome Slave
Str: 13, Dex: 13, Con: 16, Int: 8, Wis: 10, Cha: 12; HP: 12; Base AC: 12; BAB: +2; Fort: +3, Ref: +1, Will: +0; Skills: Alchemy +1, Listen +2, Swim +5; Feats: Toughness

Tecsis Sandwalker
Half-Elf Slave
Str: 15, Dex: 13, Con: 14, Int: 8, Wis: 10, Cha: 12; HP: 8; Base AC: 11; BAB: +2; Fort: +2, Ref: +1, Will: +0; Skills: Handle Animal +5, Listen +1, Search +1, Spot +1; Feats: Blind Fight

are all driven primarily by profit. Many may take advantage of a good deal offered by another stable master and be willing to buy or even trade gladiators and monsters between each other.

As far as the game Sands of Death is concerned, players are free to trade with one another in any manner in which they see fit between matches. Gladiators, weapons, monsters, in fact anything except healers (who are free-willed individuals and not slaves) may be swapped or bought outright. Some stable masters may even see fit to back up offers-that-cannot-be-refused with threats, though we would recommend such threats apply to what happens to gladiators in the arena, rather than what may occur in real life. . .

PRE-MATCH ADVERTISING

The largest stables often employ artists to produce huge banners or a myriad of paper sheets depicting their greatest gladiators and advertising when they will be fighting in any one games day. This has the effect of whipping the crowd into a frenzy as they ready themselves for what has been promised as the fight of the decade. Many may be cynical about such pre-match ploys but it has an undeniable effect upon the mob – a gladiator who has had the effect of such advertising will be greeted with howls of triumph before he has struck a single blow in the arena. As with Fame, such support of the crowd can have a beneficial effect on his fighting capability as his confidence grows with each shout.

'Are you mad?' Gildena blinked at Hamli. 'It is a sure way to become dinner for the crows.' Rosanellwyia nodded her agreement with her sister.

Hamli smiled, her heavily accented elven frustrating the eavesdropping guard, 'It is the only way to get what we want. I have the documentation I need. Regupol's arrogance and greed will do the rest. The plan will work.'

The twins stared at each other, some unspoken communication flashing between them. The human's plans had kept them alive and as comfortable as a gladiatorial slave could expect to be. If this final plan worked as Hamli seemed to think it would, the results would be more than they had ever hoped for since their capture so long ago.

'I think it would be enough to simply purchase our freedom. We have enough gold saved to do so now. Though the laws are clear, I agree that Regupol will most likely find a way to keep us, or make us pay double. There is no honour in the man.' Rosanellwyia paused for a moment. 'We will do it.' Gildena sighed as her sister spoke.

'We Fates will have the crowd on our side. We cannot fail.' Hamli's wolfish smile reminded the elves of the first time they saw her. . . strangling Lord Regupol with his own pomander.

Before a match, stable master's may advertise the event. However, other stable masters may also choose to advertise their own gladiators and very soon, a war of banners and leaflets will erupt before the match begins, with each stable attempting to outspend the others to gain the notice of the crowd. Each player must secretly write down, in multiples of 100, how many gold pieces they are willing to spend on this pre-match advertising.

The stable master who spends the most money on advertising will gain the notice of the crowd. For the next match only, all his gladiators will receive a +1 morale bonus to attack and damage rolls. This bonus may be freely stacked with other such morale bonuses. If stable masters spend an identical amount of gold on pre-match advertising, no one will receive this benefit. The monsters listed in italics on p65 may never receive this morale bonus.

WINNING SANDS OF DEATH

There are no set victory conditions for Sands of Death. Instead, players are encouraged to define their own before play begins – if they so wish. Indeed, Sands of Death may continue for a great period of time, with players gaining satisfaction from grooming their favourite gladiators. If you are having fun playing Sands of Death, don't let the completion of finite victory conditions stop you!

However, for players who prefer more strict guidelines, we recommend you choose one of the following to be the victory condition stables aim for;

Having a gladiator achieve 10th level
Gaining a predetermined amount of gold
Gaining a predetermined amount of Fame
Gaining a predetermined amount of gladiators all above 3rd level

Alternatively, you may wish to have a time-based limit – perhaps the stable closest to one of the above after a set amount of turns (games days).

SAMPLE GLADIATORS

The purpose of the gladiators presented here is two-fold. Firstly, they may be used as opponents in the Sands of Death game with which to challenge players if they have too few gladiators themselves for any given match. The wizards and sorcerers will be particularly important here. Second, they may also be used by Games Masters in regular role-playing sessions to pit gladiators against the players at a moment's notice – always useful when the group decides to enter a match you were planning they would avoid. . .

All the gladiators listed here may be armed and armoured as the Games Master wishes, or they may receive random weapons and armour as dictated on the table on p67.

Otto Grampian
Gnome Fighter 2, Beast Handler 4
Str: 11, Dex: 14, Con: 19, Int: 13, Wis: 13, Cha: 14; HP: 57; Base AC: 13; BAB: +6/+1 (+7/+2 with focus weapon), +8/+3 missile; Fort: +11, Ref: +3, Will: +2; Initiative +2; Skills: Bluff +6, Handle Animal +11, Intimidate +6, Jump +5, Perform +8, Ride +8, Tumble +4; Feats: Dodge, Expertise, Mounted Combat, Quick Draw, Weapon Focus.
Fame: 58

Taffa Swiftner
Human Rogue 1
Str: 12, Dex: 17, Con: 14, Int: 14, Wis: 10, Cha: 13; HP: 8; Base AC: 13; BAB: +1, +3 missile, +1d6 sneak attack; Fort: +2, Ref: +5, Will: +0; Initiative +7; Skills: Balance +7, Bluff +5, Disguise +5, Escape Artist +7, Intimidate +5, Move Silently +7, Perform +5, Sense Motive +4, Tumble +7, Use Magic +5, Use Rope +7; Feats: Improved Initiative.
Fame: 13

Sherba Killian
Human Rogue 3
Str: 12, Dex: 17, Con: 14, Int: 14, Wis: 10, Cha: 13; HP: 18; Base AC: 13; BAB +3, +5 missile, +2d6 sneak attack; Fort: +3, Ref: +8, Will: +1; Initiative +7; Skills: Balance +11, Bluff +7, Disguise +7, Escape Artist +9, Intimidate +9, Move Silently +9, Perform +7, Sense Motive +8, Tumble +9, Use Magic +7, Use Rope +9; Feats: Dodge, Improved Initiative, Lightning Reflexes.
Fame: 28

Lanessa Ravel
Human Rogue 5
Str: 12, Dex: 18, Con: 14, Int: 14, Wis: 10, Cha: 13; HP: 35; Base AC: 14; BAB +4, +7 missile, +3d6 sneak attack; Fort: +3, Ref: +10, Will: +1; Initiative +8; Skills: Balance +14, Bluff +9, Disguise +9, Escape Artist +12, Intimidate +11, Jump +5, Move Silently +12, Perform +9, Sense Motive +8, Tumble +12, Use Magic +9, Use Rope +10; Feats: Exotic Weapon Proficiency - Net, Improved Initiative, Lightning Reflexes.
Fame: 61

Heinfeld of the Seven
Human Wizard 3
Str: 10, Dex: 14, Con: 10, Int: 17, Wis: 12, Cha: 15; HP: 12; Base AC: 12; BAB +1, +3 missile/ray; Fort: +1, Ref: +3, Will: +4; Initiative +2; Skills: Alchemy +7, Concentration +6, Heal +4, Hide +5, Spellcraft +9, Move Silently +5; Feats: Combat Casting, Spell Mastery, Toughness; Weasel Familiar; Spells: 0 level - *Daze, Flare, Ray of Frost, Resistance*; 1st level – *Cause Fear, Colour Spray, Grease*; 2nd level – *Blur, Melf's Acid Arrow.*
Fame: 27

Blake
Human Fighter 2
Str: 17, Dex: 13, Con: 13, Int: 10, Wis: 11, Cha: 12; HP: 22; Base AC: 11; BAB +5 (+6 with focus weapon), +3 missile; Fort: +4, Ref: +1, Will: +0; Initiative +1; Skills: Climb +5, Handle Animal +6, Jump +6, Ride +8; Feats: Cleave, Power Attack, Toughness, Weapon Focus.
Fame: 23

Cita o' the Blade
Half-Elf Fighter 6
Str: 14, Dex: 18, Con: 13, Int: 10, Wis: 13, Cha: 14; HP: 42; Base AC: 14; BAB +8/+3 (+9/+4 with focus weapon), +10/+5 missile; Fort: +6, Ref: +8, Will: +3; Initiative +8; Skills: Handle Animal +8, Heal +3, Jump +2, Ride +10, Search +2, Spot +3; Feats: Dodge, Improved Initiative, Lightning Reflexes, Mobility, Weapon Focus, Weapon Specialisation.
Fame: 77

Snaggawolf
Half-Orc Fighter 4 Gladiator Champion 4
Str: 20, Dex: 15, Con: 18, Int: 10, Wis: 11, Cha: 12; HP: 86; Base AC: 12; BAB +13/+8 (+14/+9 for focus weapon), +10/+5 missile; Fort: +12, Ref: +4, Will: +2; Initiative +3; Skills: Bluff+6, Handle Animal +10, Intimidate +4, Jump +8, Perform +8, Ride +9, Tumble +5; Feats: Cleave, Combat Reflexes, Exotic Weapon Proficiency x 4, Fame & Glory, Great Cleave, Perform Bonus +2, Power Attack, Renown, Stable Status, Weapon Focus.
Fame: 97

Venga Doomspire
Human Sorcerer 5
Str: 11, Dex: 14, Con: 14, Int: 10, Wis: 11, Cha: 19; HP: 22; Base AC: 12; BAB +2, +4 missile/ray; Fort: +3, Ref: +3, Will: +4; Initiative +6 Skills:

Concentration +10, Knowledge (arcana) +8, Spellcraft +6; Feats: Skill focus (spellcraft), Improved Initiative, Empower Spell; Snake Familiar; Spells: 6 x 0 level, 5 x 1st level, 3 x 2nd level.
Fame: 46

Deloen Brightfire
Elf Wizard 7
Str: 10, Dex: 16, Con: 10, Int: 17, Wis: 12, Cha: 15; HP: 22; Base AC: 13; BAB +3, +6 missile/ray; Fort: +2, Ref: +7, Will: +6; Initiative +7; Skills: Concentration +10, Heal +6, Hide +8, Knowledge (arcana) +13, Move Silently +9; Feats: Combat Casting, Empower Spell, Improved Initiative, Improved Unarmed Strike, Weasel Familiar; Spells: 0 level - *Daze, Flare, Ray of Frost, Resistance*; 1st level – *Cause Fear, Colour Spray, Grease, Mage Armour, Expeditious Retreat*; 2nd level – *Blur, Endurance, Melf's Acid Arrow, Mirror Image*; 3rd level – *Haste, Lightning Bolt, Vampiric Touch*; 4th level - *Stone Skin.*
Fame: 68

Luis Darkmere
Human Wizard 10
Str: 10, Dex: 14, Con: 12, Int: 18, Wis: 12, Cha: 16; HP: 40; Base AC: 12; BAB +5, +7 missile/ray; Fort: +4, Ref: +5, Will: +8; Initiative +6; Skills: Alchemy +8, Concentration +14, Heal +7, Hide +7, Knowledge (arcana) +10, Spellcraft +7, Perform +6; Feats: Combat Casting, Improved Initiative, Empower Spell, Quicken Spell, Maximise Spell, Still Spell, Enlarge Spell; Toad Familiar; Spells: 0 level - *Daze, Flare, Ray of Frost, Detect Magic*; 1st level – *Cause Fear, Colour Spray, Grease, Mage Armour, Expeditious Retreat*; 2nd level – *Blur, Endurance, Melf's Acid Arrow, Mirror Image, Shatter*; 3rd level – *Haste, Lightning Bolt, Vampiric Touch, Slow*; 4th level – *Fear, Bestow Curse. Stone Skin, Wall of Fire*; 5th Level – *Cone of Cold, Shadow Evocation.*
Fame: 116

Twilight Bladevenom
Elf Fighter/Mage (Fighter 2, Wizard 3)
Str: 12, Dex: 20, Con: 10, Int: 17, Wis: 12, Cha: 13; HP: 27; Base AC: 15; BAB +4 (+5 Focus weapon), +8 missile/ray; Fort: +4, Ref: +8, Will: +4; Initiative +9; Skills: Handle Animal +7, Ride +12, Climb +6, Jump +6, Concentration +6, Spellcraft +8, Knowledge (arcana) +9; Feats: Combat Casting, Combat Casting, Improved Initiative,

Power Attack, Weapon Focus; Weasel Familiar; Spells: 0 level - *Daze, Flare, Ray of Frost, Resistance*; 1st level – *Cause Fear, Colour Spray, Mage Armour*; 2nd level –*Melf's Acid Arrow, Shatter*. Fame: 59

Gruntfuttuk
Half-Orc Barbarian 3
Str: 18, Dex: 13, Con: 14, Int: 8, Wis: 10, Cha: 8; HP: 30; Base AC: 11; BAB +7 (+8 focus weapon), +4 missile; Fort: +5, Ref: +2, Will: +0; Initiative +5, Skills: Handle Animal +5, Intimidate +5, Jump +10; Feats: Fast movement, Improved Initiative, Weapon Focus, Rage 1/day, Uncanny Dodge.
Fame: 30

Jessica Swiftdeath
Human Fighter 1
Str: 14, Dex: 17, Con: 13, Int: 11, Wis: 10, Cha: 13; HP: 11; Base AC: 13; BAB +3, +4 missile; Fort: +3, Ref: +3, Will: +0; Initiative +3; Skills: Handle Animal +5, Perform +3, Ride +7; Feats: Ambidextrous, Exotic Weapon Proficiency – Dire Flail, Two-Weapon Fighting.
Fame: 5

Jodri Deephelm
Dwarf Fighter 1
Str: 16, Dex: 11, Con: 17, Int: 11, Wis: 12, Cha: 10; HP: 13; Base AC: 10; BAB +4 (+5 with focus weapon), +1 missile; Fort: +5, Ref: +0, Will: +1; Initiative +4; Skills: Handle Animal +4, Climb +7; Feats: Improved Initiative, Weapon Focus.
Fame: 7

DESIGNER'S NOTES

In many ways, Gladiator – Sands of Death was the most ambitious project Mongoose Publishing has yet attempted and yet, it was also one of the easiest to write. Compared to the books that have gone before, all those Slayer's Guides and Encyclopaedia Arcane supplements, it was the one that changed most during its production. Originally envisioned as the definitive Games Master's guide to all things arena-bound, it quickly evolved to become more of a player's resource. Games Masters will still find all the tools required to drop entire arenas into the campaigns to be sure, but it is, I think, the players themselves who will benefit most from Gladiator.

The inspiration for this sourcebook, I think, is clear enough. All those roman gladiator film epics, with their star-studded casts and immense visions of what it was like to live in the centre of an ancient empire can have a powerful effect, none more so than Ridley Scott's production of the general Maximus. However, I was also very much aware that many roman gladiator games had already been produced in the past and, indeed, were still for sale today. We needed a new angle for our work and we soon managed to find it within the realms of fantasy. Every gladiator game book I have seen up to now concentrates on what went on during Roman times – hence you see armour types such as Thracian and Gallic, and weapons such as the Cestus and Gladius. All very evocative, but is it really fantasy? There were certainly things we did want to keep from that era though – the force of the crowd on gladiators fighting, the system of stable masters and, of course, chariot races. To make things even more difficult, I knew there would be a natural inclination to make Gladiator simply another book for Fighters. Added to that, I wanted to downplay magic (at least as far as the gladiators themselves were concerned) as I thought it rather a 'cheat' for those fighting in the arena. Instead, it was reserved for arena managers to make the lives of the gladiators far more difficult when required.

More than one of our playtesters expressed surprise at our Gladiator Champion and I was asked who in the hell would want to use such a prestige class if he was not in the arena! The response, of course, is how would you even become a gladiator champion without setting foot upon the sands of death? We never intended to do just another fighter book full of cool moves and weapons – though there are certainly plenty of those (the quad crossbow is a personal favourite). Everything within these pages is geared towards fighting within a crowd-packed arena, as you may expect in a book named Gladiator – Sands of Death. Feats that may not do much good down some darkened dungeon can have a marked effect in front of a crowd. Weapons utterly impractical for fighting hordes of orcs may become paramount when fighting a strong opponent who is very close to being your equal. This is, in essence, the line we decided to take with every part of the rules presented here. Chariots, for example, may now be purchased by adventuring parties and used in daring raids on evil encampments but they are truly weapons of the arena and it is only there that their full worth may be realised.

Last, we come to Sands of Death, the complete mini-game where players take the part of stable masters and groom gladiators to victory. This was originally seen as just a small addition to the sourcebook but as playtesting began, we started to see a rare opportunity. There is far more to Sands of Death than may meet the eye – sure, you can have fun employing the full range of combat rules from Core Rulebook I, as well as carefully building up your gladiator's skills, classes and weapons to hone them as the best combatants of the entire arena. But after just a few turns, you will also begin to see these gladiators take on a personality of their own – especially if you give them names. Very soon, whenever your gladiator uses his Taunt feat on another, you will find yourself adopting the pugnacious attitude of your protégé, challenging all opponents to 'come and have a go.' It is possible to set up long standing leagues and championships with Sands of Death and we will indeed be posting updates to enhance your games on our web site. However, that is not really the point of the game – set aside two or three gaming sessions to build up your stables but, after they are finished, keep your record sheets handy. Sands of Death is a great game to pull out and start messing around with if a regular role-playing sessions ends earlier than expected or if a member of the group cannot make it that evening.

Above all, have fun. Whether it be part of a full-blown gladiator campaign or a knockabout with Sands of Death, I sincerely hope you enjoy walking into the arena as much as we have.

'My Lords, Ladies and citizens of the Empire! For the final match of the season we have a truly rare spectacle for your pleasure, a battle drawn directly from history! You are all familiar with our beloved Lord Regupol, the hero of Valtana. See here re-created, in a reverse pyramid match, he and his men's daring escape from the clutches of the Barbarians of the Outlands that preceded the battle of Valtana which quelled the savages and made safe the western border! Lord Regupol himself will lead The Fates in the role of the escapees!' The arena manager gestured grandly to the top of the seven-level pyramid, which towered in the centre of the arena. Hamli grabbed Regupol's wrist and raised his arm high in a salute to the crowd. Cheers and shouts washed against the sides of the pyramid, a sea of adoration for the three women surrounding Regupol. The lord spoke through a clenched smile, 'Watch yourself, barbar. Do not think that the mob will save you should you harm the hero of Valtana.'

'Have you ever wondered why I do not have the auburn hair of the rest of my 'barbarian' kinsmen, Lord?' Hamli's voice grated through her teeth like a sword over a whetstone. 'Have you ever told anyone how you really escaped Valtana?'

Regupol's face went white above his smile. 'What are you on about, slave?' Small beads of nervous sweat dotted Regupol's brow.

'How you accepted the hospitality of the barbarian king, swore allegiance, took a bride, used her cruelly then slaughtered the guard as they slept unnaturally, drugged by your men.' The whip crack of Hamli's laugh startled the Lord with its venom. 'I thought not.'

'You have taken one too many blows to the head, savage, to fabricate such a tale.' Regupol's smile faltered as Hamli drew her sword.

'As we fight, documents are being given to the Regent proving that I am your daughter, as well as the gold for the freedom of we Fates. Included with the documents is a letter, written by your hand, that states should your wife and child travel through the Empire they are to be given all the considerations of a lady and a legitimate heir. Too bad you had not thought to destroy that letter so many years ago.' Hamli's speech was cut off by the blare of trumpets, announcing the beginning of the match. She let the fanfare end before she continued.

'You see, I was not *captured* as a slave, I was *sent* as your assassin.'

Lord Regupol searched for a way out of the trap he had been lead into. The arena showed no mercy to those who stepped onto its sands. He had signed a contract to fight, he could not escape. The gladiator's plan was as well executed as any of his own schemings. He saw the same hopeful look on the elves' faces he had seen the day he bought them. He felt the ghostly pressure of the pomander's wand against his throat stealing his breath.

'See you on the ground, Father - if you survive.'

The Fates saluted Lord Regupol as if accepting an order. Each woman started down a separate side of the pyramid, leaving Regupol to take the fourth side as his own.

*   *   *

'They love whom they lower; they despise whom they approve.' The Regent looked away from the crowd and peered down at the three women carrying Lord Regupol's body on his shield. The crowd had gone quiet when the noble received the deathblow from one of the 'barbarians' only halfway down the pyramid. 'I wanted an afternoon's distraction, but his fop has ruined that. No matter. You three, you Fates are now free. You have earned it with your skill in the arena. What you choose to do with that freedom is up to you.' The Regent waved his hand in dismissal. 'Have the human, Hamli I believe, sent to me on the morrow. Hopefully I can explain to her that she is to be,' he shook his head, 'a lady.'

Kime handed the slaver a small pouch then walked over to the young, heavily chained slave who was trying in vain to slip his hands out of his manacles. 'Come boy, enough of that. You're coming with me to the arena stables. You've been chosen by the Fates.'

LICENCES

RULES SUMMARY

Gaining Fame

Action	Fame Bonus
Every hit that scores 15 or more points of damage	+1
Defeating an opponent	+ enemy's level or Hit Dice
On victorious side in a match	+1
Competing in a chariot race	+1
Winning a chariot race	+1 per opponent beaten
Yielding to an opponent	-3/level of surrendering gladiator
Slaying an opponent appealing for mercy	-20

Morale Bonus for Fame

Difference in Fame	Morale Bonus
1-4	0
5-8	+1
9-15	+2
16-25	+3
26-49	+4
50+	+5

Gladiatorial Feats

Feat	Prerequisite
Armour Penetration	BAB 6+
Armour Specialisation	BAB 2+, proficient with armour
Chariot Control	Handle Animal 8+
Death Move	BAB 6+
Distract	Cha 13+
Fame & Glory	Fame 10+
Fearsome Display	BAB 3+, Intimidate 6+
Improved Chariot Sideswipe	Chariot Control
Taunt	-

Mercy

Mercy check is at DC 10, modified as below;

Action	Modifier
Scored at least one hit on opponent	+1
Brought opponent to 50% or less of starting hit points	+5
If lower character level than opponent	+2 per level
If higher level than opponent	-3 per level
Fame	+10% of Fame score (round down)
Failed to score a single hit on opponent	-4

Chariot Sideswipe Damage

Chariot Sideswipe			Chariot with Scythes Sideswipe		
Damage	Critical	Type	Damage	Critical	Type
2d4	20/x2	Bludgeoning	2d8	19-20/x2	Slashing

Chariot Handle Animal Checks

Action	DC
Cutting free a dead horse before chariot overturns	10
Swapping drivers whilst chariot is in motion	10
Hitting medium-sized creature or object	15
Hitting large sized creature or object	20
Hitting the arena wall	30

+5 bonus to check if moving at base speed or slower
–5 penalty if moving at running speed.

Exotic Weaponry

Weapon	Cost	Damage	Critical	Range Increment	Weight	Type
Aclis	1 gp	1d4	x2	10 ft.	3 lb.	Bludgeoning
Bolas, 3-ball	15 gp	1d6	x2	10 ft.	4 lb.	Bludgeoning
Chakram	35 gp	1d8	x3	10 ft.	3 lb.	Slashing
Light Harpoon	10 gp	1d8	x2	30 ft.	8 lb.	Piercing
Mancatcher	40 gp	Special	-	-	12 lb.	Special
Quad Crossbow	375 gp	1d10	19-20/x2	120 ft.	18 lb.	Piercing
Spiked Helmet	25 gp	1d6	19-20/x2	-	3 lb.	Piercing
Wrist Razor	25 gp	1d6	18-20/x2	-	5 lb.	S;ashing

Sands of Death Gladiators

Race & Class	Gold Pieces
Human	500
Elf	600
Dwarf	750
Half-Elf	550
Half-Orc	800
Gnome	450
Halfling	450
Goblin	350
Hobgoblin	600
Kobold	300
Orc	600
Arena Slave	+100
Warrior	+250
Rogue	+500
Fighter	+1,000
Barbarian	+900

Sands of Death Monstrous Gladiators

Challenge Rating	Gold Pieces
1	1,250
2	2,500
3	4,000
4	6,000
5	8,000
6	10,000
7	13,000
8	16,000
9	20,000
10+	+5,000 per CR

Sands of Death Rewards

After each match, every stable that took part will earn the following amounts of gold pieces;

Each gladiator who took part – 500 gp/level
Each gladiator who used exotic weaponry – 100 gp
Each defeated enemy – 500 gp/level

Gladiators themselves retain 20% of the total amount in their purses.

Sands of Death Expenses

Expense	Gold Pieces
Gladiator	10 gp/level + 10 gp/ Gladiator's Fame
Monster	100 gp/Hit Dice
Healer	25 gp/rank in Heal
Horses	20 gp